REACH for Teenagers

REACH for Teenagers

James Garratt

Matador
Unit E2 Airfield Business Park,
Harrison Road, Market Harborough,
Leicestershire. LE16 7UL
Tel: 0116 2792299
Email: books@troubador.co.uk
Web: www.troubador.co.uk/matador
Twitter: @matadorbooks

ISBN 978 1803135 755

British Library Cataloguing in Publication Data.
A catalogue record for this book is available from the British Library.

Printed and bound in the UK by TJ Books Limited, Padstow, Cornwall
Typeset in 14pt Bradley Hand ITC by Troubador Publishing Ltd, Leicester, UK

Matador is an imprint of Troubador Publishing Ltd

Life is like, I don't know what.
Sometimes it is, sometimes not.
Confused?
Well, at least this book reveals the essence,
of some of life's important lessons.

REACH

INTRODUCTION

OK. You have recently bought this book – or maybe someone has given it to you, or you are using it at school or college?

Yes!

Good. Now that we are talking, let's keep the conversation going.

So, we are having a conversation?

Yes, if that's OK. And when I see writing in orange – I will assume that you are making a comment or asking me a question. Are you happy with that?

Well, yes – I suppose so. So, if we are talking, can I ask you a question?

Of course.

What's this book all about? Good question.

The **title** of this book is **REACH for Teenagers**. It was written for you and it's about you. The word **REACH** is an **acronym** and an acronym (as you probably know) is a word whose individual letters are the first letters of other words. And the 'other words' in this case are: **R**elationships, **E**njoyment, **A**chievement, **C**omfort and **H**ealth.

OK? Now think about your life – and how your relationships, enjoyment, achievements, comfort and health are all 'interconnected' in ways that **make life what it is**. In fact, you could say that your **R, E, A, C** and **H** are the **basic ingredients of your existence as a human being**.

1

The basic ingredients of my existence as a human being!
Well, OK.

So: developing **Relationships** (of the positive kind).

Enjoying life (whilst respecting the rights of others).

Achieving (to the best of your ability) in all walks of life.

Being **Comfortable** in life (with all that this involves).

Achieving the best possible mental and physical **health** that you can, **is what this book is all about.**

But just to make it clear. Whilst this book is about **your R, E, A, C** and **H,** you do not, of course, exist in isolation. The way you live your life will inevitably affect (in different ways) those with whom you come into contact and, **as teenagers**, you quickly come to realise that **you** have to take more and more responsibility for your own actions, your own wellbeing and, ultimately, the wellbeing of others.

We know that.

Of course, you do. So, if you are ready, let's begin.

Oh! And just in case you are thinking '**Do I really want to read this book?',** read the poem at the back of this book first. It will give you a flavour of what the book includes.

R for Relationship

When we first think about **relationships**, we tend to think about how people 'relate to', 'get along with' or 'interact with' other people. But, of course, people don't just relate to other people, they relate to **everything** that is going on around them. Indeed, our entire lives revolve around relationships of many kinds.

I can see that.

But let's begin by thinking about person-to-person relationships and how human relationships start.

Only a new mum can begin to explain the emotional and physical experience of holding their baby for the first time. From that moment on, the relationship between mum and baby develops – it has to, of course, because the child's very survival is dependent upon it.

Developing any new relationship takes time and the **special bond** between mother and father or carers and the new baby doesn't always happen immediately, but it's all part of the relationship process.

Parenting is, clearly, a very important and responsible role and parents from different cultural backgrounds and different faith groups will inevitably have their own views on how to bring up children.

I can understand that.

That said, it is widely accepted that the groundwork of relationship building takes place in the early years of a child's life, in the period known as **'the formative years'**. It is during this period (up to the age of eight) when rapid **intellectual, social, emotional** and **physical** development takes place.

Now, as teenagers, you will have already gone through the above stages, but you may have brothers and sisters in this age range and you can, and almost certainly do, help and encourage them in their development. This can be a great learning experience for yourself in lots of different ways. If you take your role seriously, you become a carer, a teacher, a role model and so on, and you gain a lot of valuable skills. Would you agree?

I would.

Relationship building, of course, is a *lifelong* process and the **characteristics, abilities and qualities** an individual brings to the process, as a result of learning and experiences, are the **building blocks** upon which relationships develop. Ultimately, therefore, the success of *any* relationship will depend (to a certain extent) upon the *compatibility* of the individuals and/or their abilities to adapt, as appropriate.

Clearly, relationships are complex and the complexity increases when you consider the diverse range of relationships in which people engage throughout life. These include within family, friendship groups, study environments, employment situations, partner relationships and people in the wider community, for example.

Relationship building in the formative years

'The **formative years**' is a fascinating subject and there are many excellent books available if you wish to (or are required to) gain an in-depth understanding of the subject. Here, we will only be taking a brief look.

Let's begin by thinking about 'intellectual development' – the **intellect** (for our purposes) can be described as '**reasoning** and **understanding**'. Intellectual development was first formally described by the Swiss psychologist Piaget in his theory of cognitive development.

That's a strange name.

It is a bit, I agree.

Piaget explained that in the first two years of a child's life, intellectual development was closely linked to a baby's physical experiences.

During the early months of life, a baby makes lots of simple **physical movements** (technically known as **motor movements**) and these include sucking and grasping.

Through these **sensory experiences**, intellectual development is taking place, as the baby begins to **reason** and **understand** what is possible.

As the weeks and months go by, a baby's **motor skills become more complex and more coordinated**, and by the second year, they will begin to solve simple **activity-related problems** 'mentally' before carrying them out.

Along the way, adults (and older siblings) all engage **in a relationship** with the child and, in return, the child 'responds' to them. The **better they do their job**, the better the progress the child will make.

By encouraging, teaching and supporting the developing child, healthy relationships should begin to develop, with all the long-term benefits that this should ensure. Every positive interaction has the potential to enhance a child's physical, social, emotional and intellectual development.

Those early years (and beyond) are precious. As teenagers, you have such an important role to play, along with parents or carers, grandparents and so on.

We know that!

Motor and intellectual development don't occur in isolation, of course. As children engage in physical play, **language**, encouraged by adults and siblings, begins to develop. Through **language**, children acquire a greater capacity to **think**, **reason** and **understand**, and, as a result, begin to experience a whole range of **emotions**.

As every parent, or carer knows, relationship building takes on a whole new meaning once conversations are possible. And as teenagers, of course, you know all about the pitfalls of **conversations** with adults.

We certainly do!

In terms of **conversations**, Piaget went on to explain how language skills develop and change with age up to adolescence and into adulthood, as we would expect. He explained, for example, how **concrete thinking** gradually evolves into **abstract thinking**. 'Concrete thinking' can be described as 'thinking that results from a child's personal, immediate needs, wants and experiences', whilst 'abstract thinking' enables the individual to generalise, analyse, extrapolate and empathise, for example.

Extrapolate!

Yes – that's the ability to predict future outcomes based on what has been previously learnt. Whilst Piaget identified specific age ranges for these developmental changes, all children's rates of development will be different. So how does this affect the development of relationships?

Clearly, the way a child is able to relate to others is dependent on the child's **intellectual ability to do so** (which is age related).

In the early years of a child's life, parents or carers almost instinctively know how to relate to their child as they are responding primarily to the child's physical needs. Once language begins to develop, things get more complicated.

Through relationships, children **learn** how to think, understand, communicate, behave, express emotions and develop social skills.

But this learning is dependent on **the way** parents, carers and siblings **engage** in communications with younger members of the family.

It's clearly important to try to get things right, since a child who experiences a loving, reliable relationship with their parents or carers is more likely to form 'successful' relationships in adulthood'.

That said, we cannot put all the emphasis on the adults' efforts. There are many different factors that have the potential to affect the progress of a child's development. For example, **genetics** (the characteristics a child inherits from their parents), the **environment** in which a child grows up (the home, the neighbourhood and the community) and, not least, **friends** and **peer group members** are also influencing factors.

So, while there are factors over which adults have **no control** and factors over which they have **limited control**, there is one thing that should be **in their control**. And that is **the way the parents, carers and older siblings interact with the children** and the **experiences** they provide for them, within the constraints of their finances and their own health.

Some teenagers are required – for a whole range of family-related reasons – to take on much more responsibility within the home than the average teenager and may fall into the category of **young carers**.

A **young carer** is a person under the age of eighteen who regularly provides emotional and/or practical support and assistance to a family member who is disabled, physically or mentally unwell, or who misuses substances.

For a parent, carer or young carer, it is important to remember that **the ability of a child to relate to others in an appropriate way**, at a given moment in time, is dependent on their **intellectual capacity to do so.**

Clearly this must be taken into consideration during **any, and every,** communication that takes place between the adults and the children. For example, it would be inappropriate to give an 'adult type' response to a child's question or behaviour, if the child was unable to process (understand) what was being said or expected.

Fair point.

Relationships enable children to express themselves in so many different ways and what they **get back** from parents, carers, siblings and other adults – a smile, a laugh, a cuddle, a particular verbal response – provides them with **information** about 'how the world works'.

They learn how to communicate with **different people** and how to behave in **different circumstances**, and they learn about other people's **emotions** as well as their own. In fact, they acquire **a whole package of social skills**, which will stand them in good stead for their future lives and relationships.

So, the simple message to adults and older siblings, when relating to young children, **try not to overreact** to what might appear to be a 'selfish' or 'unrealistic' or 'inappropriate' outburst because physical, emotional and social development is **age-dependent.**

Age-dependent?

Yes – it takes **time** and **experience** for a youngster to develop the necessary **reasoning ability** to respond or behave appropriately to a given situation and it is the adult's responsibility to help and encourage youngsters along the way.

Being a good parent, carer or older sibling is a bit like being a good teacher. The difference is that becoming a teacher can take three (or more) years of study at university. Family members don't have that luxury; they have to learn as they 'go along'. Sometimes they get things wrong and this is when everyone needs to 'pull together', help one another and care for one another.

Effective communication is the key:

Listening, explaining, encouraging and praising, as well as providing every opportunity for the children and everyone in the household to engage in the widest possible range of experiences within family life and beyond, is so important.

Effective communication only takes place when everyone feels part of the family and is allowed to engage fully in a meaningful way where opinions, ideas and suggestions are encouraged and valued.

If we can do this well, the younger children will learn how to think creatively, communicate effectively, socialise responsibly, empathise lovingly, explore with confidence and make mistakes in safety.

Becoming an adult

The above (brief) description of childhood development, has, I hope, made you aware of some of the challenges that parenting involves and made it clear that becoming a parent is a **demanding** and **hugely responsible** role. Get it right, of course, and the rewards are priceless.

I'll take your word for that!

In childhood and early adolescence, we tend to live our lives in the 'here and now' with little thought about the future, let alone the responsibilities that this will entail; or indeed the 'type of people' we will need to become. During this period, we rely, to a large extent, on our parents, carers or young carers (where appropriate) to control and influence our behaviour and thinking. As older teenagers, though, you are increasingly expected to – and want to – take responsibility for yourself.

That's true!

However, as every teenager knows, relationships between adults and teenagers, and between teenagers and other teenagers, is a minefield of potential stress, anxiety, insecurity, uncertainty, misunderstanding, anger and any number of other issues.

You're telling me!

I know because I was a teenager once. Being a teenager can be quite a demanding time; to say the least. But, of course, it is also a time of great adventure, new experiences, learning about yourself, experiencing different emotions, taking on new responsibilities and so much more.

For the younger reader (approaching the teenage years), I am reminded of the words in an old ballad (a type of song) that went like this:

"Slow up, don't rush to grow up, you'll be a woman before long, so stay a while in the Special Years, their **magic** will soon be gone." The sentiments, of course, apply equally to boys.

This delightful song is just a reminder that childhood is (or should be) a very special time where someone else looks after you and takes on most of the responsibilities, allowing you the freedom to enjoy yourself without too many worries.

So, what's your point?

Well, it's simply this. Of course, the teenage years can be a great adventure, but the adventure **doesn't need to be rushed**, so let's take it slow and let's get it 'right'.

Not least, bear in mind the following: any relationship **that's going to work well**, requires all involved to 'have **respect** for one another'.

Respect?

Yes. We can 'respect' someone for lots of different reasons, but as far as **relationships** are concerned, let's keep this definition in mind:

Respect is having due regard for the feelings, wishes, rights and traditions of others.

With the above in mind, consider the following.

Time for some honest reflection.

To describe individual human beings as unique is not unreasonable because there are countless different **factors** that make us **what we are and who we are**. I wonder, however, what it would be like if we were **not unique**, but all exactly the same?

Think about it. If we were all exactly the same and we were all equally nice, equally fair, equally clever, equally happy and so on, would the world be a better place? I don't know, but it could be an interesting topic for conversation between a few friends. Something a bit different to talk about.

Back to reality

We are unique, of course, and this uniqueness can both benefit and disadvantage us in our relationships with those we are close to and those we hardly know.

Because our relationships occupy such a large and important part of our lives, making the most of them has got to be beneficial, not only for our own wellbeing, but for those around us. Would you agree?

Of course.

Good.

So, with the above in mind, take a look at the following lists, which identify some of the characteristics that can **aid** or **disadvantage** us in our relationships – I'm sure you could add many more examples.

Positive characteristics	Negative characteristics
Considerate	Arrogant
Caring	Unreliable
Loving	Dominant
Reliable	Aggressive
Honest	Impatient
Humble	Negative
Gentle	Lazy
Compassionate	Argumentative

The thing about people is that they are all so very different. There are the optimists and the pessimists, the confident and the shy, the quiet and the loud, the sensitive and the brash, the selfish and the generous – and so it goes on. Add to this any number of the characteristics listed above and you have one heck of a complex individual.

Furthermore, the characteristics that we develop throughout our lives can be affected by so many different factors – not least, our own upbringing.

I know that there are lots of children growing up in homes where the parents or carers don't always behave in the best possible way towards one another or the children.

Sometimes, these adults didn't experience the best possible upbringing themselves. Growing up in difficult circumstances can be tough. For some children, the experience can be a great character builder, but for others it can cause all sorts of problems. Growing up in a stable, happy family environment does not always bring out the best in people, of course, because life's ongoing challenges and experiences can have a profound effect on anyone's behaviour.

None of us are perfect!

No wonder 'getting on with other people' can be a struggle sometimes. And we don't always do or say the right things. With this in mind, give some thought to the following situations. No need to say anything – just give each situation some thought.

We don't always get things right (do we?) and sometimes we make a mistake that hurts or offends someone else (don't we?) So, do you find it easy to say sorry? Do you find it easy to forgive?

You relate to someone in a pleasant manner, but they react adversely towards you. In these circumstances, it's not unnatural to respond in an equally 'offhand' manner. Is this an ideal way to behave?

Having your own opinion about 'things' is clearly important to your **self-confidence**, but making **negative comments** about someone else's likes, dislikes or appearance, for example, can be hurtful and offensive. What is your opinion on this?

In a successful relationship, it is important that all individuals (involved) **feel valued**. Being **listened to** and having someone **show an interest in you** indicates that **you are valued**.

Do you agree?

Of course.

It's not all about me!

It's a strange thing, **but upsetting someone we are close to** (family members, for example) is sometimes **easier for us than upsetting a close friend or relative.**

That's all very well, but it's not really fair. As a teenager, you may feel – rightly or wrongly – that the adults sometimes just 'don't understand you' and this can lead to arguments and all sorts of other problems.

Picture the scene: teenage daughter arrives home late, having failed to let someone know that she was at a friend's house in the next street. Adults have been sick with worry. Daughter didn't 'get it'. An argument ensued; everyone was shouting at everyone else. The baby upstairs started to cry!

However, with a little thought and a little more consideration, things could have been very different. Do you agree?

Well, yes.

Relationships in the family home are so important. Get this 'right' and, with guidance from responsible grown-ups, chances are you'll be OK and will be able to deal appropriately with the many different types of relationships you will experience in the coming years.

The problem is, and I'm siding with you here—

Oh, that's nice!

It's not always easy to be in control of your emotions especially when things don't work out the way you want them to, or think they should.

But nobody learns to drive a car without making mistakes – and navigating life and going through the 'becoming-a-young-adult' **learning process** is far, far more complex than learning to drive a car.

One of the mistakes that **some** teenagers make is thinking that they always know what they're talking about, when, in reality, they often don't.

Oh, thank you very much!

You're welcome! But it's an easy mistake to make. After all, as teenagers you **lack experience** – you **can't help it** because you haven't **'been there, done that, got the T-shirt'**, as it were – but you think you have.

Well, if you say so!

Adults do tend to have more life experience than you do. They usually have more worries and concerns to deal with, too. When things go wrong in the family, it's most often the adults' responsibility to sort things out.

I suppose so!

In fact, being an adult is not an easy job sometimes. So, the message is: go easy on the adults. Play your part in creating a harmonious atmosphere when you can, in the home and outside. Is that fair?

Yes, OK.

Peer pressure and its consequences

People in general tend to feel **more comfortable** when they associate with 'like-minded' people. Having similar beliefs, views, opinions, expectations and so on enables them to blend into the group and contribute 'like-minded' behaviours. This has its advantages for some young people. For example, it can protect them, to some degree, from criticism and snide comments that others (within the group) might make. It can give them influence within the group – notoriety and authority, sometimes.

To be *different* or to stand out from the crowd tends to make the individual feel **uncomfortable** and this is where peer pressure can be so powerful.

Peer pressure – pressure from close friends or acquaintances – can often override one's **natural tendencies** and you end up doing something you might not normally do or want to do.

Situations like this are tough for teenagers because they want to feel accepted and to be part of the crowd. They may fear rejection if they don't fit in and even fear that they might be bullied if they walk away.

The best advice I can give is this: try to choose friendship groups based on your own values and do this earlier rather than later. Tough choices made early could well protect you from difficult situations.

Peer pressure is not always bad!

Of course not. Observing and recognising other people's **good choices** and **behaviours** can often help to redirect your life choices and behaviours. For example, observing someone's enthusiasm in the classroom might encourage you to work harder at school yourself. Similarly, talking to *like-minded* individuals can often help you to recognise your own abilities and encourage your own self-confidence. It's your choice; but it's a very important one!

I wasn't just thinking of school things!

I know. Not wanting to appear different when you are out with friends can make you feel **uncomfortable** sometimes, **yes**? And that's understandable. **But** being with 'the wrong group of friends' can make you feel **even more uncomfortable**, if their attitudes and behaviours conflict with yours.

For example, you might be encouraged to do things you wouldn't normally choose to do, like smoking, taking drugs, stealing, vandalising property, bullying, racially or sexually abusing others, engaging in unwanted sexual activity and so on. Are these the behaviours of responsible young people?

Of course not.

Some people can be quick to criticise others because of their dress sense, their weight, their appearance and so on. Is that something to be proud of?

No, it's not.

Being aware of what makes us 'who we are'.

It's not uncommon to hear a teenager say, **"I'm old enough to make my own decisions"** – and I understand why this comment is often made. After all, towards the end of adolescence, most young men and women are becoming 'independent thinkers'.

Thank you!

But, of course, along with 'making your own decisions' comes **responsibility**. Just remember: in any relationship situation, if someone challenges your behaviour, you may need to 'stop to think' and maybe recognise that **you** have made a mistake – sometimes this happens in the classroom environment.

What are you saying?

Well, it really is important to recognise and learn that the way **you** behave, both in the classroom and out of school, can have both positive and negative effects on others – and, in extreme cases, can result in serious consequences.

It's not always easy (I know) to see ourselves as we really are, or as other people see us, or to understand that our behaviour might affect others in unintentional ways. Sometimes, however, we may be perfectly aware of how our behaviour will affect others and some will thoughtlessly pursue these intentions – some of these issues will be discussed later.

I know it's stating the obvious, but the fact is that relationships are successful or not mostly as a result of the 'ingredients' (the characteristics) that the participants bring to the mix. However, human beings are individuals and so **the mix** that works in one relationship may not work in another.

Even so, at its most basic level, mutually beneficial and successful relationships have their foundations in the four Cs: **Communication, Compassion, Compromise** and **Commitment**.

Communication should allow ideas, suggestions and concerns to be exchanged freely between all.

Compassion is the response one individual makes to another where suffering or anxiety is effectively 'shared', which can help to relieve an individual's suffering.

Compromise should ensure that all parties are 'comfortable' with the outcome of any decisions made.

Commitment is essential to ensure that trust is maintained at 'every level'.

To achieve the above, however, a further essential 'ingredient' is required: **empathy**.

Empathy is an awareness of the feelings and emotions of others. Only by being able to imagine ourselves in someone else's situation, can we truly begin to understand the reasons for their thoughts and actions.

Disability, discrimination and my responsibilities

Anxiety is a normal reaction to the challenges of adolescence, as we have already discussed. Teenagers with a **disability**, however, are more likely to experience anxiety than their peers. Life can be tough for all of us and sometimes things become just too difficult to deal with. Maybe you just feel unable to make the effort, unable to motivate yourself – it's just too much trouble.

Of course, some people are much better than others at coping with demanding situations and may not recognise the above scenario, at all. But now, let's take this scenario to another 'level' and instead of talking about being **unable**, let's consider being **disabled**.

When the average non-disabled person thinks about disability, chances are that blindness, deafness, being wheelchair-bound and maybe some form of learning disability comes to mind. But just to clarify things, a person has a disability if they have a physical or mental impairment that has a long-term adverse effect on their ability to carry out normal day-to-day activities – and being a teenager at school is part of normal day-to-day activities.

You may not be aware of this, but your school is required to implement the Equality Act 2010, which protects the rights of those with a disability. As **a teenager** at secondary school, **you have responsibilities, too**. You are expected to treat all people with respect and your school will ensure that all forms of prejudice and discrimination are taken seriously and dealt with equally and fairly.

With the above in mind, consider this. Most of us, with the exception of the extreme extrovert, don't like to stand out too much or appear different from friends or peers. For a disabled person, however, standing out is something that is a fact of life.

But like the rest of us, **personality-wise**, there will be the optimist and the pessimist, the confident and the shy, the quiet and the loud, the sensitive and the brash, and so on.

So, your point?

Well, my point is this: whilst an individual with a disability might struggle sometimes with *normal day-to-day activities*, they, too, want to be part of the same crowd.

With this in mind, consider the following: It's a cold wet winter's afternoon. A wheelchair-bound pupil has been looking forward to watching the Sports Day events on the school's playing fields. In the excitement, they get left behind in the changing rooms. There's no one about. What do they do? Shout for assistance (rather embarrassing)? Struggle to get their wheelchair down the ramp (rather risky)? Being part of the crowd is not always easy!

In your very busy teenager life, how often do you give any thought, or show awareness, to those around you who may have a disability?

Maybe you are disabled. Could you make any suggestions (to an appropriate staff member at your school) that could make life for a disabled person less difficult and allow more inclusivity?

Loneliness

You would think that a teenager would be the last person to experience loneliness – after all, being young and in a busy school environment must be the ideal circumstances to meet and make friends. But, of course, it's not that straightforward.

Shyness, low self-esteem (not valuing your own ideas or opinions), self-consciousness, lack of confidence, feeling misunderstood and so on can all result in **loneliness**.

Companionship is so important – we all need someone to **relate to**; to chat to, to share our concerns with, to plan activities with, to do things with, to laugh with, to cry with and, if appropriate, to be romantic with. In other words, to **share** and **experience** life with. It's not surprising, therefore, that when **a relationship is lost or damaged**, loneliness can begin to take hold.

There are, of course, numerous different factors that can contribute to the onset of loneliness: 'petty squabbles' (within friendship groups), being bullied or racially abused, going through a break-up and so on.

Adolescence can be a harrowing experience at the best of times, but **loneliness** and the **loss of companionship** that ensues can result in feelings of insecurity and a loss of self-worth and these are so important in influencing the **mental processes** that are responsible for the way we think and respond to life's situations.

The mental processes?

Absolutely. Happy relationships during the teenage years are so important in promoting self-confidence and for establishing a general sense of wellbeing, and for going forward in life to achieve one's desires.

As life goes by, and with every new experience, we all learn more and more about ourselves and discover our own **personal identities**.

A psychologist might describe 'personal identity' as a person's **self-image**, which includes the beliefs they have about the kind of person they are and how this differs from others.

Some of the more **'positive'** characteristics that could be used to describe an individual's 'personal identity' are:

honest, trustworthy, supportive, generous, kind, respectful, communicative, fair-minded, generous.

But no one is perfect and maybe you can identify some **negative** characteristics in your own personality.

That's a big ask, isn't it? I mean, the negative bit?

True, but sort this out now and you can be sure that it will benefit you in future relationships of every kind. You might find it interesting to give some thought to your own 'personal identity' <u>now</u> and think about how you apply the **four Cs and empathy** in your current relationships – personal and casual.

Reconciliation and ending relationships

Sometimes, relationships come to an end or need to be ended.

Not the happiest thought!

True, but the end of a friendship or a romantic relationship may sometimes be seen as a good thing because there was no 'spark' (as it were) or the 'chemistry wasn't there' or, quite simply, it 'wasn't right for you'.

Even so, in the best interests of all concerned, ending a relationship should ideally be amicable. Would you agree?

Not necessarily. Sometimes the people involved are not worth talking to.

I understand that but it's only fair (if you are the one ending the relationship) to try to explain to the other person or persons **why** you need the relationship to end.

After all, often, when someone wants to end a relationship, their partner is the last person to know and it can really hurt, and **they** may want to know why.

True.

With this in mind, give some thought to the following:
Do you think it's a good idea to finish a relationship by text or email?

That depends.

True. I know that having a face-to-face **conversation** with the individual with whom you wish to end a relationship may prove difficult or distressing for both parties, especially if they **plead** with you 'not to do this' or **get angry** with you and so on. If you suspect that this might occur, **what measures could you take** to help resolve the situation, whilst still having the face-to-face conversation?

And what about ending a relationship by **phone**? If you decide that this is the best way forward, what **concerns might this cause** for yourself and for the other party?

Tough questions.

Break-ups happen all the time and for a whole range of reasons. It's so important for you to understand that as we get older – particularly during the teenage years – we change. Our interests change, our plans change, our expectations change and, yes, believe it or not, the kind of people we want to settle down and spend our lives with will change.

So, if you face a difficult break-up, try to stay positive. Find things to do to take your mind off your immediate concerns. Whilst doing this, though, don't be tempted to do anything 'rash' – anything that might, in the long run, put you at risk or cause different worries.

Relationships online

If you are fairly old like me – which you're not because you're a teenager – you would remember a time when neither mobile phones nor the Internet existed and neither, of course, did social media. Today, however, these technologies are an accepted part of life.

The thing about **social media technology** is that it only becomes social media **when humans make use of it**, and the way it is used determines its advantages and disadvantages to society and the individual.

As history and everyday life has shown, human beings can be incredibly creative, inventive, generous, caring, loving and so on, but equally they can be destructive, cruel, hateful, antisocial and even evil. Give unpleasant individuals the tools of social media and they have the potential to become even more unpleasant.

The humble text

There is no doubt about it, the ability to communicate quickly and relatively cheaply by text is a real asset of social media.

When used to send quick messages such as, "Sorry, I'm running a bit late – be there at around 9.30" or "Thanks for the lovely birthday card" and so on, our busy lives become so much easier to manage and, as a result, potentially more enjoyable.

Then there are those short communications that can reassure mum or dad or your carers that you are OK and what time to expect you home. Texting and verbal communication using a mobile phone enables friends to be in touch and keep in touch at any time, to provide a sense of security or, simply, just to talk. Unfortunately, even **a simple text** has the power to hurt, cause anxiety or fear, or be misinterpreted and cause unintentional distress.

We know that!

Of course, you do! Some people use texting to **deliberately** cause hurt, anxiety and fear. There is **nothing clever nor worthy of respect** in this kind of behaviour, but it is **not** uncommon and **bullying**, which we discuss in the next section, is an extreme example.

Beyond the text

The Internet, of course, has provided the world with a vast communication network allowing people to communicate with friends and family, locally and across the globe, and on many different platforms including Facebook, WhatsApp, Instagram and so on.

We can also play online games and do **so much more**. I'll leave the **'so much more'**, of which I have minimal knowledge, to the experts – the young people.

However, in addition to the hurt that can be inflicted on others, social media can **'damage you'**.

Damage me?

You know it can! Social media, despite its many benefits, can be very **addictive** and one of the serious consequences of this addiction is **time**.

You will all be different; with different interests, different priorities, different reasons for being on the internet or on your phone, and the **number of hours per day** occupied by social media, which can be excessive.

If the **time** factor is not addressed, eye strain, disturbed sleep, social withdrawal and resulting irritability have the potential to cause long-term health problems. Is this something you have given any thought?

Not recently – well, maybe.

Of course, some forms of social media have the ability to create a **false sense of reality**. Meeting people on-line and being drawn into innocent communications with a stranger, who may not even be the person they say they are, is an obvious example.

We know that.

I'm sure you do. **Just be careful.** It can be so easy for someone who has experienced a relationship break-up, for example, to become vulnerable to the attentions of an **apparently** well-meaning individual online.

Now, let's give some thought to how social media can affect others.

Bullying

In 1971 (long before you were born), the BBC ran a series adaptation of the 1857 Thomas Hughes novel, *Tom Brown's Schooldays*.

Flashman was the notorious school bully. His **cruelty** to others and particularly Tom had no limits. His behaviour was inhumane. **Flashman was one of the older boys**, someone who should have been setting a good example to the younger lads, but he gained enjoyment and notoriety from his appalling treatment of others.

Tom suffered extreme distress and physical injuries (which he eventually overcame) and, ultimately, witnessed Flashman's embarrassing removal from the school.

In Tom's day, of course, there were no mobile phones and no internet, but bullies still intimidated people and caused emotional distress and physical injury.

Bullying has happened throughout history. Today, people in all age groups, from primary school children to elderly adults, may experience bullying.

So, why do people bully others? Why do some individuals choose to be **so cruel**? To be **cruel** is to wilfully cause pain or suffering to others whilst feeling no concern for the victims. In a moment, we will consider the 'why', but first let us think about **you**, if you are being bullied now.

For many teenagers, life is difficult enough under normal circumstances. Add to this the often distressing, frightening and threatening behaviours resulting from the actions of a **bully** (towards you) and the natural response is to want to hide and withdraw.

The mind then begins to get **tormented** with thoughts of **self-criticism**. Stress and anxiety cloud the judgement and questions such as 'What's wrong with me?' begin to be asked. But it is not you who is at fault – *it is the person who is bullying you who has the issue*.

In Tom's day, the bully was likely to be within 'shouting distance' or closer. Today, of course, the bully may be sitting many miles away, without anyone else knowing what they are doing, trying to intimidate you by instant messaging, e-mails and so on. They could post stuff about you on sites that others read and this can lead to group bullying.

So how should you deal with online bullying?

The general advice is **not to read any of the bully's messages**. Delete them straightaway – yes, straightaway. I know that it can be tempting to message back with a nasty response, but resist the temptation. You'll only become more involved! Instead, block the bully's communications as soon as you are able. To learn how to do this, type 'How to block emails' into a search engine or speak to your IT teacher. Do the same for text messages.

Bullies like to make you feel that they are powerful and you are weak. Show them that you are **not** by ignoring them and isolating them. You can do this because, when we need to, we can all find inner strength.

As mentioned before, all schools must implement the Equality Act 2010, which protects the rights of those with a 'protected characteristic' – bullying is included. As an absolute minimum, therefore, you must tell someone who you trust and, together, decide how to proceed. Ideally, you and your trusted friend should seek help from your class teacher or headteacher. Even if the bullying takes place out of school, your school will be able to help.

Any kind of behaviour aimed at hurting an individual or group, either physically or emotionally, is a behaviour that I'm sure most young people deplore.

Low-level, face-to face-bullying, where an individual is 'targeted' repeatedly and often over a long period of time, can be as damaging as being bullied on-line. The behaviour can be motivated for any number of reasons, including jealousy, racial prejudice, physical appearance, religious beliefs, gender, sexual orientation, disabilities, special educational needs and so on.

Whilst the bully may see their behaviour as 'just a bit of fun' or 'fooling around', it can have long-term health implications for the victim, including severe anxiety, depression and, in extreme cases, result in the victim taking their own life.

Bullying is clearly an extremely serious practice that has no place in our schools, workplaces or society in general. It is everyone's **responsibility** to do all they can to eradicate this inhumane behaviour.

Low-level banter, when just 'fooling around' with friends, can easily degrade into comments that become upsetting or offensive to a sensitive individual. Just because the perpetrator doesn't believe that their comments are offensive, the comments can be seen as **very personal** to the recipient.

So, every responsible young person has a duty (I believe) to help their friends (and others) who are being bullied to feel OK and to feel safe – and, where appropriate, to support them in getting help to stop the bullying.

Just a few words now about the 'why' question. Why do people bully? Why are some people prepared to be so cruel? Research suggests that individuals develop bullying tendencies as a result of life's circumstances, home background, peer pressure and so on.

A bully may not know why they behave in this way. Maybe it's insecurity, anger or frustration that drives their behaviour, but – almost certainly – their behaviour will 'damage them'. For example, it is suggested that persistent bullies are at high risk of developing long-term mental health problems and find it difficult to form close social and emotional relationships. **If nothing else**, this should encourage a bully (or potential bully) to rethink their behaviours.

Racism

Let me tell you a story I heard, about 'a moment in time' on a battlefield somewhere in France, during the Second World War.

In the heat of battle, two soldiers witnessed a horrific event, too dreadful to describe, and without thought for their own safety they ran towards the 'situation' and together dragged a fellow soldier away, just in time to save his life.
The soldiers were of the same rank and of a similar age. The only visible difference between the two men was their colour. One was **black** and the other **white**.

During that war and others before, men and women from all over the British Commonwealth, and from many other countries around the world, including the USA, came to the aid of Britain and the free world. They fought, often in appalling conditions, and in their tens of thousands **died** to protect our freedom and democracy.

Can you imagine? Can you even begin to imagine the sheer horror that soldiers endured in countless different 'theatres of war' during the Second World War?

I feel that it would be disrespectful of me, having no related experience, to try to imagine or describe such an experience, so, instead, I will relate an event that was once related to me.

"In front of us was a beautiful green landscape full of colour, birdsong and the scent of wild flowers; but within just a short space of time it was transformed into a desolate mud-drenched terrain filled with the smell and sight of death and mutilation.

Soldiers, black and white and from many different cultures, became traumatised by the events unfolding before their eyes and the mind-numbing, deafening sound of gunfire and explosions. The dead and wounded lay unattended and those who survived had no consolation since they knew they would face the same again tomorrow – and the next day, and the next, for as long as the madness continued."

In this context, I am reminded of the words often spoken at Remembrance services: "When you go home, tell them of us and say, for your tomorrow, we gave our today." (John Maxwell Edmonds, 1916).

So why am I describing these wartime events? What have they got to do with racism?

I was wondering that!

Well, simply this.

If people from different races, cultures and backgrounds can support and care for one another in times of great adversity, why should things be any different in peacetime? Racism is so destructive. Not only can it affect the victim's mental and physical health, but it can have a devastating effect upon local community life and on society itself. Unfortunately, racism has become so entrenched in some areas of society that 'decent people', who are not at all racist, somehow fall into the trap of racist behaviour.

The causes of racism and its consequences are hugely complex and these pages can only scratch the surface of this hugely important issue.

But let's not forget that many of the **descendants** of those incredibly brave and selfless men and women (referred to above), who fought and died for our freedom, live amongst us – and, to our shame, experience racial prejudice, discrimination, antagonism and abuse.

Furthermore, people from all over the world, from different races, ethnic backgrounds and cultural groups contribute their skills, knowledge and enthusiasm in service of our nation.

At this point, a 'potential racist' might be interested in giving some thought to a number of theories related to racism.

One of the psychological theories of racism is that the perpetrator (the racist) fears that:

Their 'security' is being threatened.

Their 'importance' is at stake.

They are 'at risk of losing control'.

This suggests a lot of **insecurity** on the part of the racist individual.

I suppose that racially abusing a footballer **from the security** of the terraces, therefore, supports these ideas.

Another theory suggests that the racist has a deep-seated and probably unconscious feeling that they are not 'good enough' (they have a low opinion of themselves). By abusing someone who is perceived to be 'better than themselves' or 'different' somehow deflects from their own inadequacies.

It is not easy for any of us to accept that we have 'imperfections', 'deficiencies' and 'weaknesses', but the fact is that we do. Those who are realistic about their own weaknesses and strengths tend to be happier people.

The 'need to belong' is a basic human requirement and a powerful motivating force. It is suggested that for some people, who find it difficult to form meaningful personal relationships, joining a group that gives them an 'identity' and a 'common cause' has a big attraction and, sometimes, racist behaviour takes place in groups of like-minded individuals. That said, there is nothing positive about racism. It is an ugly and destructive activity.

Whatever the motivation for such behaviour, there are no long-term benefits for the perpetrator. Indeed, research suggests that the long-term effects of such behaviours can include torment, regret, shame and so much more. **If nothing else**, this should encourage a racist (or potential racist) to rethink their behaviours.

Sexism

As previously stated, 'Our entire lives revolve around relationships of many kinds'. **However, as important as relationships are to the orderly functioning of society and to the potential benefits of all**, we can (as the past few pages have highlighted) either benefit or disadvantage our fellow human beings in many different ways **through our choices of behaviour.**

Relationships are the **building blocks** that create the **fabric of life**. Relationships are only successful, however, when respect, trust and security exist within the relationship.

For many, though, respect, trust and security does not exist:

It does not exist in bullying. It does not exist in racial prejudice and it does not exist in the **everyday experiences** of many **women and girls** across the land who experience **sexism**.

Sexism is the oppression, abuse and mistreatment of women and girls by *dominant males*, sometimes based on the belief that one sex is intrinsically superior to another. At its most extreme, sexism includes sexual abuse, harassment, rape, and other forms of sexual assault and violence.

Harassment, intimidation, aggression, physical or sexual violence **perpetrated by a man or boy** towards a **known** woman or girl, or by a predator towards an **unknown** victim, **is an abhorrent act. Fear of such behaviour** causes anxiety and distress to tens of thousands of women and girls on a daily basis on our streets, in our schools, clubs, universities, workplaces and in the home. Beyond the fear, an **actual physical act** can result in physical injury, mental trauma and, in extreme cases, it can tragically result in death.

It has to be acknowledged, however, that there are millions of potentially decent, law-abiding, caring and considerate men and boys whose natural instinct is to help and protect others. **So why do some men and boys carry out such horrific acts on women and girls?**

An answer to the above question is hugely complex and would likely require different experts to provide a range of answers. But we **all** have a responsibility, I believe, to attempt to make progress in addressing **this extremely distressing issue**, even if we feel that our potential to bring about change is limited – **though I don't think it is**.

So, let's make a start by giving some thought to the following.

We become what we experience, don't we? It's not surprising that the experiences we have as a child influence our future behaviours. Introduce a child to books in the early years and read them stories, and most often the child will be motivated towards learning to read themselves and become good readers.

Show displeasure and provide reasoning for why a child shouldn't steal a sibling's favourite toy (for example) and the child will begin to learn what is, and is not, acceptable social behaviour.

In the same context, learning from the adults in the family home, by example and explanation, about how to behave respectfully towards members of the opposite sex is an important parental or carer responsibility, isn't it?
If you experience inappropriate behaviour at home, **whilst you may not feel able to speak out**, you should not allow this behaviour to influence the way you behave, should you?

Social norms?

It is suggested, in some research related to sexism, that **social norms** relating to the way girls and boys are **expected** to think, feel or act can influence future behaviour that **might** contribute towards inappropriate **male** sexual behaviour. Parents or carers have a major part to play in this context.

Whilst modern parents, with the above in mind, may try hard to treat their children (girls and boys) 'equally', this can be difficult. For example, mum puts on make-up in the morning, but dad doesn't. It's not surprising that the daughter wants to do the same – after all, she is female, just like her mum.

Boys at play tend to gravitate towards physical activities involving 'rough and tumble' including play-fighting, which many parents probably accept as a 'boy thing'. Girls, whilst equally happy to engage in 'rough and tumble', tend to engage more frequently in play that involves a gentler approach.

But does the male tendency to pursue physical activities necessarily lead to male aggressive behaviour in adulthood? A great deal of trolling through the research would be needed to try to answer this question.

Gender roles

As the teenage years approach, a whole new set of demands take over as **gender roles** begin to dominate the thought processes. **The origin of gender roles** is complex and is not consistent across different cultures. Gender roles change (within society) as **the influences that influence them** become more dominant.

Take great care, therefore, and do not allow internet content, the media in general or people (often older than yourself) to encourage you to do anything that feels 'uncomfortable' or 'wrong', even though the suggestion is that these are today's norms.

Peer pressure

The attitudes of others and situational pressures can often override an individual's normal inclinations, natural behavioural characteristics and values to a detrimental degree. So, whilst a young man or boy (on their own) is less likely to verbally intimidate a woman or girl, it can be very different when out with a **group of friends**.

I know that it's only natural to spend time with other people who have similar interests to you. If, however, behaviours that you are uncomfortable with, or disagree with, begin to take place, **it's time to speak out** and show your disapproval.

After all, boys, you are not 'sheep', are you? You don't have to follow the crowd, do you?

The above is an example of where a young man or boy can really demonstrate that **strength has value**, unlike the example that follows.

Some do because they can!

Men and boys, as a result of their physiological characteristics, are usually bigger and stronger than women and girls and therefore **can** aggressively dominate the opposite sex for that reason alone.

To use these 'advantages' to intimidate or harm a woman or girl is clearly a **shameful way to behave**. There is nothing macho, nothing brave and nothing worthy of respect in this kind of behaviour. Would you agree that this is an example of **strength** being a **weakness**?

Let's value our differences

Women and men **are different** and these differences, whilst having an obvious biological purpose, **encapsulate a wealth of other values and qualities**. If these are allowed to **flourish with respect, trust and security, and without prejudice**, in all aspects of life, society should benefit on many different levels. Indeed, it is these **incredible differences** that have the potential to make human life so rich and special.

You haven't said very much recently, have you?

No...!

I can understand why. Bullying, racism and sexual abuse are not the easiest of topics to talk about. If you are **being affected in any way**, in any of these areas, **talk to someone you can trust** and get the situation resolved. You deserve to be happy; you deserve to be well and you deserve to feel safe.

Relationships of a 'less obvious variety'

A relationship, by definition, is 'the way in which two or more people or things are connected, or the state of being connected'. There are also many **different types of relationships** that people engage in on a daily basis that might not immediately come to mind as a relationship – a few of these are described below.

In school and in wider society, we all (young and old) expect to be treated with respect, but equally we have a responsibility to treat others with respect. Remember this definition: **'Respect is having due regard for the feelings, wishes, rights and traditions of others'.**

Life is unpredictable. No one is immune to misfortune, accidents or distress. In these circumstances, it is often a complete stranger who comes to our aid. It may be a 'professional' stranger, such as a paramedic, a nurse, a doctor, a police officer, a fireman, a voluntary worker and so on. These are incredible people who dedicate their lives to helping others in need or in distress. They deserve to be treated with respect, but this is not always the case.

A relationship of this kind may only last for a few minutes, but it can have lasting effects. To the beneficiary, it could be 'life-changing' or even 'life-saving'. To the professional, it can be very rewarding, but if treated badly, both physical and/or psychological damage may result.

We are so lucky to have dedicated people like this to look after us in times of need. Let's not forget how important these relationships are, however brief they may be.

Most seventeen to eighteen-year-olds learn to drive and having that opportunity is such a privilege, but even driving is a 'relationship'. **Sometimes relationships take place at a distance** and road traffic 'incidents' fall into that category.

For example, behaving aggressively, shouting through an open window or gesturing are examples of poor relationship behaviour.

Sometimes drivers behave recklessly – driving too fast or just plain dangerously, often putting other road users or pedestrian's lives at risk. However, when driving a vehicle on public roads, **you are in a relationship with other users** and should behave responsibly.

And then there are the purely **selfish road users**. There are countless examples – and I'm sure you can recall examples yourself – of where selfish behaviour puts others (and yourself) at risk.

So, remember, as a driver (or passenger), **you are in a relationship** – a relationship with other road users. Please, therefore, drive safely, respect the rules of the road and let's keep everyone safe.

E for Enjoyment

There's no doubt about it, life is complex and enjoyment can be fleeting – and sometimes it can be scarce. Sometimes it is not appropriate, because of suffering or bereavement, for example, and sometimes circumstances beyond our control (such as the covid pandemic) can have a huge impact on our enjoyment.

And then there is the unacceptable behaviour of some individuals, which can severely affect another's enjoyment.

Despite the unpleasant individuals amongst us, human beings are an incredible species. Through the senses of sight, hearing, touch, taste and smell, we are able to enjoy the beauty of nature, the activities and products of our own and other's creativity, and our interactions, with other people and other creatures.

The problem is that life, by its very nature, is complex, and our feelings and emotions can have a huge impact on our wellbeing and happiness.

It's all very well when 'things are going smoothly', but it can be very different when things 'go wrong'. It's at these times that anxiety, fear, anger, lack of self-confidence, feelings of rejection, depression and loneliness can take hold, and enjoyment takes a back seat. **It's at these times when good friends often come to the rescue.**

Friendship in the teenage years.

Some friendships made in the teenage years can last a lifetime, but often we lose touch with school friends when we leave school, go into further education or employment. **Friendships, of course, by their very nature, can be very influential.** We tend to spend a lot of time with friends and their behaviours, attitudes and beliefs can have a habit of 'rubbing off' on us (sometimes). Of course, we want to feel accepted, valued and appreciated, but this can, if we end up with the 'wrong type' of friends, result in problems down the line.

What do you mean – the 'wrong type' of friends?

I suppose the answer to this question depends on your point of view. If you are a caring person who respects the rights of others – and this includes people you don't even know – shows concern when someone is in distress, is kind, thoughtful, helpful and so on, then the 'wrong type' of friends would be those who display the opposite characteristics.

The teenage years can be a time of great insecurity; after all, 'everything' very quickly becomes your problem, your concern and **your responsibility**, and a lack of experience, which is not your fault, doesn't help.

Well, that's OK then.

OK? Maybe, but not as an excuse for poor behaviour, disrespect or any other attitudes that create problems, worries or anxieties for other people.

This is getting very personal!

Sorry, I'm just trying to help. What I'm trying to say is this: good friends are great to be with, but for all their good intentions, things don't always turn out well. **It's a communication thing** – sometimes. **Communicating** with friends should be the easiest thing to do. After all, you know them well and you know what their interests are, and what makes them tick.

So, I suppose you don't need to say very much more about this then!

Not sure it's that straightforward! Adolescence is a time of rapid change, emotionally and physiologically. From one week to the next, moods change, opinions change, expectations change and even beliefs change. So, communicating with friends can sometimes create all sorts of problems.

You make it all sound so difficult.

OK, but think about the following situation for a minute. One of your friends, who is normally very easy-going, suddenly starts to show aggressive (albeit mild) behaviours. You might, in a caring way, try to find out what's going on, but all you get back is abuse. So, what **is** going on?

Well, unfortunately, **all sorts of things could be going on. It may just be a 'growing-up thing'**, or something that has happened in your friend's family. They may be experiencing peer pressure in some context or someone is bullying them. They may be experiencing racial or sexual abuse, or they might be going through a relationship break-up and so on.

The above has, kind of, illustrated how fragile friendships can be during the teenage years and goes to show just how important and precious friendship relationships are.

Socialising with friends, of course, is a great way to let down your hair, have fun and develop new friendships, but socialising is **not for everyone.**

There are lots of reasons why some people struggle to socialise in a group situation. Some young people simply **lack confidence**; they may feel that they will have nothing to say and nothing to contribute. Others may prefer to remain **emotionally detached** as a means of protecting them from the anxiety and stress that social interactions might evoke.

Whilst being perfectly understandable, the above can impact negatively on one's social life and potentially affect one's future relationships, work prospects and, not least, one's mental health. **So, as a friend; when help is needed, be there to listen, help and support.**

Respect.

As mentioned previously, any relationship **that's going to work well** requires all involved to have **respect** for one another. You may remember that you were asked to keep the following definition in mind:

'Respect is having due regard for the feelings, wishes, rights and traditions of others'.

I'm sure you would agree, therefore (if you accept the above definition), that life is likely to be more **enjoyable** for everyone involved if their wishes, rights and traditions **are respected.**

Let's consider this now – and let's start with home life.

It's not surprising that communications between **yourself** (a teenager) and the **adults** at **home** can sometimes become fraught, because the 'things' experienced by the adults, when they were teenagers, were often very different to the 'things' that teenagers experience today. So much has changed – not least technology, with all the advantages and disadvantages that this entails.

Young people do tend to have different ideas, values and beliefs to their parents or carers, but this has always been the case **because society changes with every generation.** Teenagers today tend to have – and expect – more independence from the adults and this can cause the adult all sorts of anxiety. Adults, however, because of their life experiences, do tend to be more aware of the 'pitfalls of life' and try to guide, advise and protect their children as much as they can.

With the above in mind, consider the following:

You have been invited to go to a friend's birthday party in the next village and you have also been invited to stay overnight. Your friend's parents will not be there overnight and there will be a spare bedroom in which you can sleep.

Of course, you will want to enjoy your evening, but your parents will want to enjoy their evening, too, without having to worry about you. How might you approach the above (or similar) situation in a way that might help to alleviate the adults' worries? What might you **say** or **do**?

Respect in the classroom

Going to school is a legal requirement in the UK and its purpose is to prepare young people for their future lives in society and the community.

The many different subjects taught have their content chosen to provide a range of information and experiences within the academic, artistic, practical, sociological and political arenas.

The problem – and I completely understand this – is that not everyone will have the same interests or the same abilities to make the most of the lessons they attend.

That's true.

This, however, should not be an excuse **for anyone** to 'mess around' or be 'disruptive' in class.

Your teachers deserve to be spoken to politely and treated with respect, and your **fellow pupils** should be allowed to learn without their progress being affected by inappropriate interruptions.

I know that in every classroom there will be individuals who find the content or the skills required *difficult* and there will be those who find the content or the skills required less difficult, but if classmates are prepared to cooperate and help one another, everyone should gain more enjoyment from their lessons and make the progress of which they are capable.

It may be stating the obvious—

You often say this.

Yes, I know. I must try to say it less often. However, what I am about to say is not only 'stating the obvious', but you can confirm it yourself by visiting any number of related internet sites.

So, what was I about to say? Oh yes; the better your educational **qualifications**, the better your chances of acquiring a well-paid job when you leave school or getting into a further education course of your choosing.

Having respect for your teachers and having respect for your fellow pupils will, ultimately, (and this is a fact) be reflected in **the respect you have for yourself** in the coming years.

Respect in your personal relationships

Towards the end of the teenage years, **intimacy** is likely to play an increasing role in your personal relationships. Since **Relationship and Sex Education** (RSE) is required to be delivered in all secondary schools and covers a **huge range of issues** (both physical and emotional), I will leave this topic mainly to your teachers.

It is important to be aware, though, that more than fifty per cent of teenagers do not have intimate relationships in their teenage years. Even so, of all the relationships in which young people do engage, there is nothing potentially more fulfilling, precious and enjoyable than being in a successful intimate relationship. I say 'potentially more fulfilling, precious and enjoyable' because it requires, in full measure, the **four Cs** (Communication, Compassion, Compromise and Commitment) and a large helping of **empathy** to make the magic happen.

Any successful relationship requires **good communications**, but an intimate relationship requires a **very special kind** of **communication**. The words, the expressions, the sentiments will be (or should be) very loving, caring and respectful. The way you **communicate**, of course, is dependent on the way **you feel** or are **made to feel**, in a given situation and these **feelings** are reflected in your thoughts, emotions, reactions and behaviours.

But just to complicate things a little more (a lot more!), your thinking, emotions, reactions and behaviours can be affected by a multitude of factors including:

Your gender, your age, your cultural beliefs, your sexual orientation and, of course, your upbringing and past experiences.

Anyway, for now, let's think about **emotions** for a while

In life, in general, you can expect (obviously) to experience both positive and negative emotions, but within an intimate relationship you might expect to experience the emotions that promote **enjoyment**, including excitement, anticipation, contentment, pleasure and so on.

The problem is that first dates, like any new experience in life, can require a bit of getting used to. After all, you don't necessarily know what to expect or how to behave.

Getting to know a prospective new girlfriend or boyfriend takes time – and gaining trust is so important, **including understanding and respecting each other's values and boundaries**, which need to be adhered to.

Of course, there may well be **times of distress** or **misunderstanding** in a relationship and sometimes **compassion** has a role to play.

Compassion is the response we have when confronted with another's suffering and we have the desire and motivation to relieve that suffering.

As honourable as compassion is in a relationship, however, **you need to be on your guard** to ensure that you are not 'tricked' by another person's disguised suffering or disappointment, in a way that allows you to be taken advantage of or, worse still, abused.

Compassion, when lovingly expressed and genuinely deserved, is at the heart of a mutually respectful, loving relationship, but just remember that abuse is when you begin to feel scared or controlled by the person you are with.

If your boyfriend or girlfriend is being physically or emotionally abusive in any way, including over the phone or the internet, this is relationship abuse. If you are seriously concerned and are unable to resolve the issues on your own, speak to an adult you can trust as a matter of urgency.

Compromise

In life, compromise is generally an everyday accepted requirement (unless we are very selfish).

Compromise is an agreed solution to a problem where people with differing opinions or requirements accept a 'middle-ground' approach that 'kind of' works to everyone's satisfaction.

As far as teenage relationships are concerned (let alone intimate relationships), compromise can be a tough ask.

Why so?

Well, firstly, a teenager's feelings, expectations, desires, attitudes and everything else can change on a regular basis and that is to be expected.

As I'm sure you are aware, the teenage years are a time of growth spurts, puberty changes (when you mature sexually) and so much more. Some changes occur very rapidly and others more slowly, and changes can occur at different ages, even within the same gender.

Girls tend to mature earlier than boys (become fully developed in both mind and body) and all of these factors come into play when 'going out with' and 'relating to' others in an intimate relationship.

OK, we get that.

So, **compromising** and making a decision that is acceptable today, may not be acceptable tomorrow. Relationships in the teenage years, therefore, should be enjoyable (yes) but should not involve behaviours that could compromise future standards, happiness or outcomes that you might, in the future, regret.

Compromise in a relationship is most often arrived at when there is open discussion, clear understanding, mutual respect and empathy. It is often said that **no one should compromise if to do so means you have to go against your beliefs or values.** What do you feel about this advice?

That's good advice.

Commitment

Commitment in a relationship (a dedication or obligation that binds an individual to their partner) has huge benefits, not only in promoting a long-term, happy, successful relationship, but for the wellbeing of any children that may 'come along'.

Whilst many teenage intimate relationships are often of short duration, commitment is equally important. **Commitment ensures that the time spent together provides a sense of security and, in this context, commitment requires trust, reliability and exclusivity.**

Empathy

Gossiping with friends about a new boyfriend/girlfriend is only natural, **but some things need to be private**. Would you agree?

Well, yes!

And what about the adults? How important do you think it is to tell your parents or carers that you are 'going out with someone' and what exactly do they need to know, and why?

Depends on how well you get on at home.

Fair point.

It's good to see teenagers from different cultural backgrounds 'going out together' – and clearly being aware that each other's beliefs and values may well be different makes empathy so important. Would you agree?

Of course.

So, just to conclude, **if you accept that Communication, Compassion, Compromise and Commitment are essential elements of a successful relationship, then you have to conclude that empathy has a big part to play.**

After all, we are social animals. We have to get on with other people and we can only Communicate with, have Compassion for, Compromise with and have Commitment to others if we truly **understand** their feelings, thoughts, attitudes, behaviours and so on. Would you agree?

Yes, when you put it like that.

Just one more thing (slightly different but very important) before we leave this chapter.

Climate change and its consequences are something young people are rightly getting very passionate about and a lot of the problems, **believe it or not**, are **related to enjoyment**.

Buying new shoes, clothes, electronic gadgets and every other conceivable product in the shops and online has become an everyday **enjoyable** pastime for millions of people on a daily basis (in the more affluent nations of the world, that is) and we **enjoy acquiring, having and using** these products.

What's wrong with that? This chapter is supposed to be about enjoyment.

True, but unfortunately, the manufacturing, the use, the transportation and the disposal of any and every product has consequences for our planet's health, and the health and wellbeing of every creature and every person living on earth today and in the future.

If you have any doubts about the above statement, type the following question into a search engine: 'How does the manufacture of a product affect the environment on a daily basis?'

I remember a time when products **lasted much longer than they do today** and some manufacturers 'decided' that they had to find a way of encouraging the buying public to keep buying their products, so **inbuilt obsolescence** was cleverly introduced.

Inbuilt adolescence! No! The word is **obsolescence**.

Yes – **Inbuilt obsolescence**. Products were designed to have a **limited life** by ensuring that they **failed** more readily. In addition, manufacturers **change the design of their products** regularly to make the previous products appear 'out of date'. Clever **advertising** is used to persuade the consumer that they would **really benefit** from buying the latest products.

But you can't just blame the product designers, manufacturers and advertising – **you** have a responsibility to make a difference by changing **your buying habits**. As 'everyday teenagers', you should all give some thought to the following questions:

Am I buying too many products as a result of my **wants** rather than my **needs**?

Do I really need **to upgrade to the latest product design** so regularly?

Should I buy more **locally manufactured products** to reduce the transport 'carbon footprint', as well as supporting the local economy?

Should I be **more aware and more selective** with regards to the materials products are made of?

How can I avoid **impulse buying** (buying things that I don't need)?

It really is our **responsibility** – all of us, young and old. Along with governments, scientists, inventors, engineers, manufacturers and producers doing what they can, **we need to act now**. If not, you, your children, your grandchildren and your great-grandchildren's lives will inevitably suffer as a result of our **over-indulgent** pursuit of **enjoyment** through material possessions. Sorry, but it needed saying. OK! OK!

A for Achievement

Parents love to see their children **achieving** and achievement for the child is a great **motivating factor**. Put simply, achievement is having succeeded in doing something that we were previously unable to do or doing something better than we previously could.

I like that definition.

Oh good. I like it, too. Anyway... **Picture the scene:**

a four-year-old wobbling and swerving as they manage, for the first time, to ride their bike without stabilisers. What joy for the child! What joy for the adults!

Growing up is a time of great change and the things that motivate a two-year-old, a five-year-old, a ten-year-old to achieve will be very different to what motivates you (a teenager) to achieve.

Well, that's obvious.

During the early growing-up years, the home environment and role models like mum, dad, carers, grandparents, teachers and celebrities etc. are likely to be the biggest contributors and motivating influences.

And we play our part, too – the older siblings.

Sorry, of course you do. In the teenage years, as you know, friends can have a significant 'influence' on an individual's attitudes, expectations and behaviour – and the consequences are **not always positive**.

How do you mean?

Well, the problem is (as we have alluded to previously) 'navigating adolescence' can sometimes feel like 'baking a cake without a recipe'.

You say some strange things sometimes.

I know, but being a bit light-hearted can 'make the medicine go down' a bit more easily (sometimes).

There you go again!

OK, let's get serious again. Lack of experience can cause all sorts of problems, so remember that mum and dad or your carers are likely to be around to help you and they usually have a lot more experience than you do – on most areas in life.

I suppose so!

The teenage years have the potential to be full of excitement, adventure and new experiences, but your **education** is just as important, of course. **Deciding what you want to do when you leave school can be a tough one for any teenager.**

Thoughts like 'What do I really want to do with my life?' come to mind and 'What would I really enjoy doing?' This will inevitably lead to thoughts regarding subject choices at school and speaking to a careers advisor might be a good starting point.

And then there are thoughts like 'What am I really good at and what can I realistically achieve?'

OK, what's this leading to?

School Days – the Teenage Years.

So, this is what it's leading to!

You may have heard it said that **'School days are the best days of your life'.** For some young people, this will be true, but for others, it will be quite the opposite. There are countless reasons why school has unpleasant **memories** for some and very unpleasant **experiences** for others.

Racism, bullying and sexist behaviour (which we have mentioned earlier) are obvious examples of the kind of experiences that can make school life difficult, frightening and, sometimes, intolerable.

Every school pupil is, of course, an individual and the experiences they have, and the way they respond to them, will also be very different.

When I was five years old (many years ago), I had a minor illness that resulted in me **missing most of my first year at school.** As a result, I got off to a very poor start with my reading. One of the consequences of this is that, even today, I am a slow reader. Years later, when I was at secondary school, I was **viciously beaten around the head** by a teacher **for a very minor incident**, with which I had no connection.

Did this really happen?

Yes, it's absolutely true. **I also experienced some physical bullying after school, when cycling home.** But whilst I didn't fight back (there were too many of them), I didn't allow it to intimidate me. I simply cycled home a different way from then on.

Several years later, when attending college, a lecturer **who appeared to enjoy picking on students** (including myself) **who couldn't always answer her questions** made me feel very uncomfortable. So much so that I decided not to attend her lecture anymore. I do realise, of course, that it is not always easy to 'remove oneself' from a difficult situation – and in **school**, this is not really an option at all. In this case, I was nearing the end of the course and so my lack of attendance didn't affect me too much.

I am telling you these stories to simply illustrate that I do understand the struggles and pain that some pupils experience, but I did enjoy school, college and university very much because I enjoyed learning.

OK, let's talk about you now.

You're at school; you may really enjoy school; love learning and have ideas about what you want to do with your life in the future. I'm not going to say very much more about the well-motivated, organised pupils like you, because chances are you can sort things out for yourselves – fantastic. Alternatively, whilst you might enjoy some subjects, others you just can't stand, right?

Maybe!

Maybe you really struggle with reading or find maths and science just too difficult; maybe you 'mess about' in lessons to keep in with your friends or just to cover up for your embarrassment.

I understand all of that **and chances are it's not necessarily your fault**. All sorts of things, even things you have not been aware of, can have been responsible for your difficulties.

But I urge you to seek help from your teachers – let your school help you. Don't miss out on your education. **It's your future that's at stake.**

My future! Why should I learn all these different subjects at school? I'll never need most of that knowledge after I've left.

OK, let's try to answer that one. Firstly, believe it or not, you will, in the future, find a lot of the knowledge you've gained useful. You may not (necessarily) require it in your chosen career, but the knowledge you gain at school will help you throughout your life in numerous different ways. From socialising to running the family home, 'knowing stuff' will enable you to talk knowledgably, calculate effectively, plan creatively and enjoy variety.

But the **real value** of school learning is not the knowledge, it's the **learning processes** that you go through: the thinking, the analysing, the problem-solving and the creativity. **These are 'transferable skills' that will stand you in good stead for the whole of your life.**

OK, I get the message!

So, don't be afraid to say that you don't understand. Most teachers love to help pupils who want to learn. Do some learning at home. Ask your teacher for some extra learning resources. Make an effort. With every bit of progress you make, you **will** gain more and more confidence.

Even in lessons you don't particularly like (and in other situations throughout life), **listen** and take an interest because – as this poem states:

Only by **listening** will you **hear.**

Only by **hearing** will you begin to **understand.**

Only by **understanding** will you gain the **skills**

required to go forward in life and **achieve your desires.**

But now we need to consider the 'can't-be-bothered' pupils.

Maybe you can't be bothered because you genuinely feel that you are 'no good' at anything, but that's not true (and this belief has consequences).

It's **so easy** to 'mess about' in class and to disrupt the lesson. I understand that, in a way, you probably feel that you are being successful at something – and yes you are. You are successfully affecting other people's learning. Maybe that doesn't bother you, but you need to realise that you are also being successful in damaging your own future.

If you are not a 'can't-be-bothered' pupil, you don't necessarily need to read the next bit, but you might have a friend who would benefit from your input (as it were).

I understand that you may be a poor reader, find writing stuff down too difficult, find some subjects just too hard or boring, hate feeling embarrassed because of your lack of understanding and so on. **And I know that it's only natural to gravitate towards others who have similar experiences to yourself – and this will only make the situation worse.**

So please, have the courage to try to break free. I know it will take **one 'heck of an effort'**, but you'll feel so good when the effort begins to pay off.

Why not talk to a friend about making an effort together? You don't need to tell anyone else. Surprise yourself (and everyone else) with your progress.

Discovering your strengths

Achievement almost always requires effort and effort requires **motivation**. By motivation, I mean 'a reason for doing something or behaving in a particular way'. I know that for some teenagers, 'doing well at school' is really not your priority. For many different reasons, some of which have been discussed previously, you are happy just to get by and survive.

Yes – just survive!

I once heard a teacher say **"Everybody is good at something"** and I agree. So, what I would like you to do (if you think that you are only capable of surviving) is as follows. Think of **something** that you **are good at** and write it down on a piece of paper.

Write it down!

Yes – being able to **see your thoughts** written down can be really useful sometimes.

Now, think very carefully about **why** you are good at this 'something' and then write down all the reasons **'why'**.

For example, it may be because you practiced doing it; because someone helped you to improve or because it interested you.

Oh, and don't include in your list 'Because I enjoy doing it', because whilst enjoyment can **motivate** you to **do something better**, it usually works the other way round. That is; **being good at something** is what creates the enjoyment.

So, what does all this prove?

Hopefully it goes some way towards demonstrating that **knowing you are good at something** proves that you have the **qualities** to enable you to **be good at other things, too**. It's just a matter of being prepared to put in the effort.

You may not be the best in the class and sometimes the not-so-pleasant individuals might tease you about this, but let it be 'water off a duck's back'. Ignore it; don't let someone else's immaturity damage your future.

There you go again – 'water off a duck's back'. Well, I suppose it's quite apt.

It's not surprising that past and present experiences (both physical and psychological) tend to 'cloud your judgment' and influence your current thinking, **but let's not forget what achievement achieves.**

Not only will you have fulfilled your original aim, but you will also be a **different person** – more confident, more able and more self-assured.

Achievement is multi-faceted, so even if things go wrong along the way and you don't quite 'make it', you will have gained many new skills and experiences that will stand you in good stead for the future. **Achievements are the building blocks that promote human progress.**

We are all unique individuals – and from birth through to adulthood, the 'influences' that triggered and nurtured our achievements will also have been unique, but **you owe it to yourself** to do the best that you can and be the best that you can.

So, now, let's consider 'how you can achieve better'.

How to achieve better (for those who feel that they are not doing as well as they could)

I know it's stating the obvious, but the **way we think** and **what we think about** affects the way we **feel about things**, which, in turn, affects the way we are likely to **react, communicate** and **behave** in different situations.

That's quite a mouthful!

Clearly, **thinking** is a very important skill (to say the least) and **thinking 'differently'** may well be what's required sometimes to enable you to **achieve better**. Indeed, the writing activity you did earlier 'kind of' suggests this. Relying on old ideas, old objections and old behaviours can get you nowhere, sometimes.

Thinking skills, of course, develop and continue to develop during the growing-up years, through childhood and adolescence – and, to a certain extent, our upbringing and past experiences mould our thinking.

But it's never too late to **learn to think better** – and to do this usually means to **think differently**. Let's be clear, good thinkers are **not born that way; thinking is a skill**. With this in mind, complete the thinking activities below.

More activities?

You don't need to write anything down (unless you really want to), but keeping a record of your thoughts can be very helpful. You'll be surprised at how quickly you can broaden your mind and expand your thinking by simply being able to '**look at your thoughts on paper**'.

Many of you **know what you want to do** when you leave school. You may have chosen to go into further education, do an apprenticeship, find employment and so on – **fantastic**.

For those of you **who have not thought this far ahead**, then maybe it's time to start thinking! Visiting your school's careers advisor is an obvious first step. You can then begin to **think about** the options available to you and what you need to do in preparation.

It can be very easy to assume that **because you find a particular subject difficult**, this will always be the case. If this is what you think, what could you do to begin to change the situation? **Give it some thought** and don't just consider obvious possibilities – **think differently**.

Sometimes, past failures can be a real 'put off', which can result in you never making any changes. Don't dwell on the past; plan a different approach. What might this approach be? **Think about it** and work something out.

Don't assume that the way other people study will necessarily work for you. Of course, you will need to go to the same lessons as everyone else, but you may need to do some additional study. Your school's learning resources may be excellent, but some of them may not meet your needs. Where might you find alternative resources and who could you ask to help? Don't just ignore this question; **do something about it**.

The above may all sound like **a lot of thinking** – and even a lot of effort and hard work, too – but it will all benefit you in the future. **And that's guaranteed.**

C for Comfort

When you first think about the word 'comfort', a state of **physical wellbeing** probably comes to mind. But, of course, comfort relates equally to our **thoughts and our emotions**.

Ask any of your friends what gives them comfort, or would give them comfort in their lives, and their answers would probably be very different. They would be different because they are **individuals**, having grown up in different circumstances, with different personalities and beliefs and different expectations of life. Even so, most people would probably identify the following as general indicators of comfort:

1. Being free of physical pain.
2. Being free from worry or disappointment.
3. Being free from stress or anxiety.
4. A general feeling of wellbeing.
5. Being relaxed in company.
6. Being at ease with oneself and one's actions.
7. A feeling of contentment.
8. Being in a happy relationship.
And for those with a religious belief:
The knowledge of a Spiritual Comforter.

Of course, **life is a roller coaster of events** and because we are physical and emotional beings, **discomfort** – the opposite condition to any of the comfort 'indicators' listed above – is an everyday possibility.

Whilst it is natural to strive for pleasure and try to avoid pain and disappointment, some people struggle more than others when faced with uncomfortable situations and they don't necessarily respond in the most constructive way.

So, your point?

71

Well, my point is this.

Anyone can experience discomfort at any time for any number of reasons and often it takes the intervention of **someone else** to help to relieve the individual's suffering. Words of comfort are so important in situations like this – and sometimes action is needed, too.

Friends, of course, can have a big part to play. For the recipient, it is often the **realisation** that someone has **noticed** or **acknowledged** their **discomfort** and is **prepared to help** that begins the healing process and they begin to feel better.

Well, that's obvious!

Good. I'm glad you're with me on this.

Anyway, at its most basic level, we can all relate to **comfort in action** that we might, on a daily basis, be required to demonstrate. For example, your brother or sister falls and cuts their knee, or a friend is in distress as a result of an argument or recent bad news. These are circumstances to which we instinctively and willingly respond.

But life's distresses can be, and often are, far more serious and demanding of our attention and interventions – and at these times, a greater input might be required. So, let's step back in time for a while and consider our own comfort journey.

Our own comfort journey?

The comfort journey

Young people emerging from childhood, well before the teenage years, begin to **question things** about **themselves** and **life in general**, which may never have crossed their minds before. These thoughts can sometimes be quite disturbing. Do you agree?

I do!

Stepping out of the relative **comfort zone** of early childhood, with its routines, reliability and the protection of parents or carers, can create all sorts of new thoughts, worries and anxieties for young people.

For some children, who have grown up in homes where the adults haven't always behaved in the best possible way towards one another, or their children, the transition can more demanding.

It all starts to get more complicated when **concrete thinking** (the reasoning based on what you see, hear, feel and experience) begins to change to **abstract thinking** (when the ability to analyse, extrapolate, generalise and empathise takes over).

With increasing maturity, therefore, **one's responsibilities towards others** is 'expected' to be taken to a new level with regard to the way you might affect another's feelings.

Think about it. **You** can make someone **feel comfortable** (or not) by the way **you react, communicate** and **behave** towards them.

Equally, of course, **someone** can make **you feel comfortable** (or not) by the way **they react, communicate** and **behave** towards you. It's a communication thing. Knowing how to communicate appropriately and effectively is a valuable skill to have.

Being a **responsible human being** – and having due regard for the **feelings of others** – takes practice, experience and, of course, **empathy** (being able to 'imagine yourself' in someone else's situation and understand the reasons for their thoughts and actions).

You've explained empathy before.

OK, sorry! As I was about to say – in the teenage years, when there are so many new things to learn and understand and where experience can be in short supply, it can take **time** to 'get things right'. I know I don't need to tell you this (but I will, anyway), feeling **comfortable** in any relationship **is very important**.

So, be on the lookout for the kind of behaviours and personality characteristics (within a new relationship partner) that **you** are going to be happy with. Look at the list below and think about which characteristics are likely to make **you** feel comfortable in a new **friendship** relationship:

considerate, dominant, caring, lazy, humble, impatient, compassionate, arrogant, honest, argumentative.

OK, I understand what you are getting at, but it can take time to get to know someone new.

Absolutely.

When not being comfortable can be helpful.

How can not being comfortable be helpful?

Let me explain.

It may not be something that you think about on a daily basis, but all sorts of uncomfortable things help us to stay safe or protect us from harm as we **react to them** via the **senses** of sight, hearing, touch, taste and smell. Hot things, bad smells, loud noises – that kind of thing.

But in this section, I'm thinking more about **uncomfortable emotional experiences** and how they can protect us, warn us or encourage us to behave cautiously sometimes. For example:

There are those **uncomfortable feelings** you sometimes get as a result of your **own actions**. You can think of this as a kind of **alarm mechanism**. Selfish behaviour, impatience, jealousy, anger and so on are behaviours that do us 'no justice' and which almost always have a negative impact on others.

But, of course, feeling **uncomfortable** in these situations is very much dependent upon your own **moral values** and your personal views on issues relating to 'right and wrong'. The foundation and development of these values takes place during childhood and adolescence, but as a young adult you are expected to become an **'independent thinker'**, fully responsible for your own decisions and behaviours.

An 'independent thinker' – I like that.

Independent, yes, but sometimes with the **help** of the **conscience.**

The conscience?

Yes, the inner voice that questions our thoughts and actions. Whether you believe that **conscience** is the result of **the rational mind making moral decisions** based on past experiences and influences, or is **the voice of God** prompting our actions, **how you respond** or **behave** is **ultimately up to you.**

So, it's still my decision?

Yes, but making the 'wrong' decision or taking the 'wrong' course of action – **resulting in someone else's distress or suffering** – can leave anyone feeling ashamed and very **uncomfortable.**

Being **honest** with ourselves, **recognising our errors**, being prepared to **learn from past experiences** and, where appropriate, **apologising for our behaviour** should help both the offended party and ourselves feel better.

And then there are those situations when **causing discomfort** can be a **'defence mechanism'.**

You must be joking.

No. If someone's **response** to being told **the hard truth about something** results in a better 'long-term' outcome for themselves (albeit initially resulting in a short-term period of stress or anxiety), then the strategy **may** be considered as valuable.

This is a tough one and will always need to be handled with great care and compassion. Both parties will need to think carefully about the potential consequences of any proposed actions. For example:

A friend has recently become acquainted with a member of the opposite sex who you **'know to be'** not the most reliable or trustworthy. You have concerns for their wellbeing. As a friend, you feel that you have a 'responsibility' to warn them. **But how do you do this** without seeming to interfere, or get involved, in something which your friend might view as 'none of your business'?

Can 'not being comfortable' with your actions sometimes be justified?

Not sure about this.

I suppose it depends on the situation!

I agree.

When comfort can be self-defeating

Another strange heading – what can this be about, I wonder?

You may never have tried to learn to play a guitar, but if you had you would probably have found it really **uncomfortable** to 'contort your fingers' around the fretboard when playing chords – and also how painful the fingertips become before they toughen up.

It can be so easy (in a situation like this) to go for the **more comfortable option** of 'not bothering', but by persevering, the fun and pleasure you will get over the coming years will all have been worth the effort and the discomfort.

That's all very well, but what if you are not interested in playing a guitar?

Well, you have probably guessed, by now, that I'm going to talk to you about **schoolwork** and **other achievements** in life that you can miss out on – if you allow discomfort to put you off.

OK, let's hear it!

There will be, in life, countless activities, through choice or necessity, that will require you to accept discomfort if you want to 'make progress'. Going for the easy option is OK – if you don't mind **missing out**!

Missing out?

Yes! In the previous chapter, the importance of schoolwork was discussed, related to **knowledge** and the **learning processes**, and I acknowledged that finding things difficult, being embarrassed, peer pressure and so on can be a real 'put off'.

But feeling uncomfortable shouldn't really be an excuse to **miss out on any aspects of your life**. I know that 'excuse' is not the best word because it can be so tough sometimes, but please, seek help, find a way – don't let discomfort be a barrier to your future success in life.

The following scenarios are just two examples that illustrate how **discomfort** can result in someone **'missing an opportunity'**.

You would really like to learn to play tennis (better) this summer, but compared to everyone else in the club, **you're rubbish** (well, so you think), so it's not worth going.

You really fancy that new girl or boy who has just joined your school, but you are fearful of approaching them because you couldn't take the **rejection** if they ignored you.

Sometimes, overcoming your fears (because that's what they are) is to **'face your fears'**. Easier said than done, I know. So, try this: make a decision to act, think about what **'could go wrong'** and decide **how you could deal** with the **going-wrong bit** – if it happened. Then do it!

Comfort in action – the kindness factor

Have you ever thought about – **really thought about** – what **kindness is** and how **important it is as a human response?**

Kindness is a type of behaviour marked by acts of generosity, consideration or concern for others, without expecting praise or reward.

Friends may have any number of different worries, anxieties and concerns related to family problems, relationship issues and even health concerns, for which you may feel totally inadequate to provide help. But one thing that doesn't require a specific 'qualification' is **kindness**. You may have heard it said that 'kindness is love in action'. But **what is love?**

There is, in the Christian Bible, a 'definition' of **love** that powerfully portrays the depth and breadth of this potentially powerful human response and experience. **Whether you have a religious belief or not,** the list of **qualities** expressed in this passage (from 1 Corinthians 13) has applications in all experiences of life. It reads as follows:

"Love is **patient,** love is **kind.** It does **not envy,** it **does not boast,** it is **not proud.** It does **not dishonour others,** it is **not self-seeking,** it is **not easily angered,** it **keeps no record of wrongs.** Love **does not delight in evil** but **rejoices with the truth.** It **always protects, always trusts, always hopes, always perseveres."**

So, whilst **kindness itself doesn't require a specific 'qualification'**, the Bible's 'expression of love' provides a 'check list' that could, I suggest, be used by anyone to help them to 'deliver it'.

With this in mind, give some thought to the following situation.

The teenage years are inevitably a time of change. In addition to the expected physical changes, behaviours change, beliefs change, needs and wants change and, not least, the way one sees the world changes. It's not surprising, therefore, that friendships change, too. **Friends who you are happy to be with this week, you may not feel the same about next week.**

Not wanting to associate with (or be friends with) a particular individual, for whatever reason, means that sometimes you have to **'let them down'** – and this can mean letting them know that you don't want to see them anymore. Chances are the individual is going to feel upset and offended, to say the least.

Consider, for a moment, how you might (if the above situation arose), responsibly and without causing too much distress, **explain to someone** that you don't want to spend so much time with them.

Keep in mind the sentiments expressed in the Bible verse above and don't forget empathy, which is clearly so important when trying to relate to someone who might have 'issues' or be 'difficult to be with' sometimes. I know that this is a tough one, but just isolating someone in an 'offhand' way, with no explanation, **is the opposite of kindness.**

The comfort journey

From 'distress to feeling better', the comfort journey will, of course, be different for each individual and in every different circumstance. And let's not forget that the **input** from someone **trying to help** can sometimes **complicate matters**, because it's all too easy to get things wrong and even make things worse.

So, how to proceed?

The first obvious question you will need to ask is **'What's wrong'** and then it's a matter of **listening**, because only by **really listening** will you be in a position to think about how you might be able to help. To encourage someone to explain what's wrong and express their worries, you need to show that you are **interested**.

But be careful – **asking the 'wrong kind of questions'** can cause distress and confusion. And what about **coming up with your own solutions and giving advice**? This can be tempting; after all, you are trying to help. But you need to be very careful, as *your* way of dealing with a given situation can be very different to theirs.

Agreeing or **disagreeing** with the **reasons for someone's distress** can also be tempting, but this can cause all sorts of issues.

Sometimes, when trying to help someone in distress, you can find yourself **in conflict with their opinions or behaviours**. You don't want to be seen as **being judgemental** (disapproving), but you do need to maintain your own values.

Sometimes an individual in distress can feel **so low** that their self-esteem (confidence in one's own worth or abilities) is badly shaken. This is another area of concern.

Just a minute – we don't seem to be getting anywhere with this.

I'm glad you're 'on the ball'. So, here are a few points you need to keep in mind:

Listening is very important and the individual needs to know that you are genuinely interested and willing to help.

As far as **questions** are concerned, they need to be **open-ended** (questions that encourage the individual to **think about** and **explain** how they are feeling, rather than just giving 'yes' or 'no' answers).

Avoiding situations that are likely to cause extra stress is very important, too, so avoid **coming up with your own solutions** because this is more likely to **complicate matters**.

Similarly, **agreeing** or **disagreeing** might sound like you are **being supportive**, but how can you be sure (not having been in the given situation yourself) that your opinions are valid.

Being **supportive** is very important, of course, but do this by encouraging them to talk about the situation and to consider what **they** would like **you** to do to help.

The bottom line is this: keep all of the above in mind and do your best to help the individual to feel better. Even if their values conflict with your values, **don't be judgemental** – these are issues that you might discuss with them in the future.

For now, your aim should be to **build up their confidence** by giving them **support** to help them feel better. The way you do this, of course, will be dependent on many different factors, known only to you.

Unless you are an expert councillor (which you probably aren't), you may well say the wrong things sometimes and the individual might react negatively towards you. So, it's up to **you** to remain **calm**, to respond **gently** and to be **patient**.

I think I can do that.

I have confidence that you can.

H for Health

As we begin this chapter, I want to introduce **you** to **yourself.**

Introduce me to myself! Are you kidding?

No, I'm not kidding – just bear with me. Most likely, the first thing you will be aware of **when you wake up in the morning is your physical body**. You may feel warm and relaxed, too warm maybe, or you may feel cold. You may even be experiencing some physical pain in some part of your body.

And then there are those thoughts. I can't begin to suggest what they might be because you are yourself – an individual with your own problems, expectations, desires and responsibilities.

When you get up, maybe you **look in the mirror**. Again, you **see what you see**, and you **feel whatever the visual image suggests to you.**

I'm not sure what this is all leading to.

Don't worry, I'll explain. The human body is an extraordinary structure of the highest level of sophistication and complexity. Whether you believe that everything on Earth was **created** by a **spiritual being**, or its origins and current form came about by chance and an **evolutionary process**, you are still **you** and you exist within a design **worthy of respect.**

A design worthy of respect?

Absolutely. Respect is 'a deep admiration for something (or someone) elicited by their abilities or qualities'.

To fully respect **the human body**, therefore, requires an understanding of its 'abilities and qualities'. Unless you (in your future career) work in the medical profession, this knowledge, understandably, will be fairly limited. Even so, looking after your own health, by knowing what is good for you, or not, **is** and **will be**, throughout your life, **largely your own responsibility**.

At school, for example, you are likely to receive lots of really important health-related information using a whole range of different resources. In addition, your school may invite speakers in to talk to you on a whole range of issues, either based on their own experiences or as experts in their particular field.

And, of course, nurses, doctors, surgeons, physiotherapists, occupational therapists, councillors and so on will always be available within the NHS to help you to stay well, keep safe and to recover from illness.

Your health is a lifelong responsibility and the 'information' you will need to be aware of and understand will come from many different sources throughout life.

You might find the information that follows useful.

The air that we breathe

With so many things to think about as we go about our busy lives, it's not surprising that we tend **not to think about** our health – either physical or mental – until we feel unwell.

Just a minute. So, in short, what you're saying is our health is not high on the agenda until it begins to affect us?

Exactly! But this way of thinking can, **if you are not very careful**, create all sorts of long-term problems. As I have said before, 'navigating the teenage years is a bit like baking a cake without a recipe' – and, as every good cook knows, along with the recipe, you need to have an understanding of the ingredients and experience using them. But understanding and experience of life can be in short supply in the early teenage years.

Now, whilst 'understanding' (in most learning situations in life) is gained through experience, there are some situations in life where understanding through experience is far from ideal!

This is getting a little confusing. Can you explain?

Yes, I will. And I'd like to start by talking about **breathing**?

Breathing

We all take breathing for granted and rarely (if ever) think about why we do it. **So why do we breathe? What's its purpose?**

Put simply, breathing enables all of our bodily organs to work effectively. Our organs need **oxygen** from the air and getting oxygen into the **lungs** (as we breathe) is the first step towards getting oxygen to the rest of the body via the bloodstream.

But you knew this, of course, because it's something you learn about in your science lessons.

That's true.

For our purposes, I want to talk about some of the substances that can enter your body when you breathe in, **which, ideally, shouldn't.**

For example, you can breathe in someone else's 'germs' when they cough or sneeze nearby. It can also happen when walking near a busy road and you breathe in motor vehicle exhaust fumes – or it can happen when you **deliberately** inhale dangerous chemicals if you **smoke** or take **drugs**.

Coughs and sneezes and exhaust fumes are always best avoided if you can. For asthma sufferers, avoiding vehicle exhaust fumes is particularly important.

When it comes to smoking or taking drugs, however, **it's your choice** – it's not something that you 'come across' as a normal hazard of living.

I'm not going to tell you about the dangers of smoking or taking drugs, because **your school will arrange for you to receive expert advice** on these topics. My aim is to help you, **if I can**, to avoid these practices in the first place. **Your health, your choice.**

If you don't give it much thought, **smoking** may appear to be a harmless pastime, **but smoking remains the leading preventable cause of illness and premature death in the UK.** Whilst smoking has fallen significantly over recent decades, **there are still countless young people growing up in homes where smoking is seen as the norm.**

Whilst role model influences (adults in the home, for example) is one reason why young people start to smoke, **research suggest that the reasons for teenage smoking habits are complex and extend way beyond peer pressure or role model influences.**

For whatever reason (and **if you smoke**, you may well be aware of what the reason was in your case), **the health risks associated with smoking are well established.**

I think we've got the message.

If you are in any doubt concerning the health risks associated with smoking, go onto the website **'What are the risks of smoking?' – NHS** and you can read about the **multiple risks** there.

Including:

1. Lung cancer and cancer in many other parts of the body.
2. Heart disease.
3. Stroke.
4. COPD (look it up)
5. Impotence in males (look it up).
6. Cervical cancer. Women who smoke are twice as likely as those who don't smoke to get cervical cancer.

There are, of course, all sorts of reasons why a young person might smoke. Some of the comments I have heard include:

1. "It helps me to relax."
2. "I enjoy smoking."
3. "It enables me to feel part of the group."
4. "It gives me confidence."
5. "It's a social thing."

But the potential health risks associated with smoking far outweigh any short-term 'benefits' that a smoker might experience.

Research suggests that people who start smoking in their teens and continue for two decades or more will **die twenty to twenty-five years earlier** than those who never light up.

Ideally, you should never start, but if you have and you want to stop, go to the: 'Under-18s guide to quitting smoking' (NHS internet site) for **facts** and **advice**.

It's your health, your choice.

Drugs

When I was boy, I had a scooter – not a posh electric one, like those available today, just a very basic metal scooter with wobbly metal wheels and solid tyres. It was old, it was second-hand, but it was mine – **until someone stole it.** It was **my fault** because I had left it unattended when playing in the park.

It never got replaced and its loss affected me badly. It did, however,

teach me a lesson that has stayed with me all of my life:

Never risk losing something important to you, which, once

lost, can be difficult to replace.

What has this story got to do with drugs?

I'll try to explain.

There are **many different reasons** why someone might start to take drugs – **just a few** are listed below:

1. Curiosity.
2. Peer pressure.
3. Enjoyment.
4. A rebellious nature.
5. As a survival mechanism.

And with drug-taking in mind, give some thought to the following sentences – in particular, the statements in **bold text**:

Wanting to be different in the teenage years can sometimes lead to rebellious behaviour, but this can result in you **losing your sense of security.**

When you are with a group of friends, peer pressure can sometimes **reduce your sense of self identity**.

Curiosity is fine, but reckless curiosity resulting from taking unknown risks can result in you **losing your ability to make important informed life decisions**.

Many drugs can cause strange experiences, and this can create **a false and dangerous sense of reality**.

Taking drugs can sometimes be seen as a survival mechanism – a way of forgetting problems or difficult life situations – but it **will almost always reduce your sense of responsibility**.

Do any of the suggestions in bold text make you feel differently about experimenting with drugs?

Recovering from the loss of a material possession (a scooter, for example) is **nothing** compared to recovering from loss of control, poor health, homelessness (it happens), addictions (dependency on something) and so on.

Listen to the **experts** and those who have recovered and can speak to you from **personal experience** about the risks, dangers and consequences of becoming involved with drugs.

It's your health, your choice – well, at least, it should be.

Alcohol use and misuse

Let's begin with an odd question.

If alcoholic drinks (beer, wine and spirits) didn't exist, **would it matter?**

Of course, it would matter. For a start, tens of thousands of people who work in the drinks industry, including pubs and shops, would be out of work.

Good point – anything else?

It's a social thing. It helps people to relax and enjoy the company of others.

That's true; **alcohol affects brain function, changing a person's moods and behaviour.** Anything else?

I think it can have some health benefits, if consumed in small quantities.

That's true, but the facts would need checking out.

So much for the **'benefits'** of alcohol consumption. Now, let's consider some of the **'downsides'**:

I'll leave that up to you then.

Thank you very much. Well, first of all, because alcohol **can affect brain function**, it can affect:

- the ability to control behaviour, resulting (sometimes) in irresponsible, reckless or even violent actions.

- the ability to drive safely – with all the consequence this can have for those in the car and innocent others.

- the ability to avoid being 'taken advantage of' either physically or sexually.

- life expectancy – worldwide, 3.3 million deaths were attributed to alcohol misuse in 2012 (World Health Organization, 2014)

It also has to be remembered that rate of alcohol consumption, genetic risk, gender, ethnicity and body mass can all affect an individual's response to alcohol use very differently.

With the above in mind, consider the following: Whilst teenage parties are a great way to relax and have fun – and that's fine; it can be easy to lose track of time and reality when you are enjoying yourself. **So please ensure that you do not succumb to the excessive consumption of alcohol at a party.**

Binge drinking (drinking lots of alcohol in a short space of time or drinking to get drunk) is proving to be an unsafe, unhealthy pastime. **Is this something you need to think about?**

While **alcohol** is a part of life and can make you feel relaxed and accepted in company, it is still a **drug** – and during the teenage and early adult years, the **brain is still developing**. This makes the teenage brain more vulnerable to alcohol damage than the adult brain. **This is serious – look it up.**

OK, we get the message.

To make a gingerbread man or woman

I'm not a very good cook, but I do know that to make a gingerbread man **biscuit** would require me to have a **recipe** that lists the required **ingredients**, such as flour, ginger, cinnamon, baking soda, nutmeg, salt, butter, brown sugar, egg and so on.

I would also need to know the different **ingredient quantities** and **cooking times** etc. Get it wrong and I could end up with a soggy mess or an incredibly hard lump.

You might well be wondering why I am telling you this.

I am, actually. But I'm getting used to your weird interventions!

Well, have you ever heard the saying **'You are what you eat'**? Well, it's true. Our bodily tissues: muscles, bones, ligaments, tendons, skin, hair and all of our internal organs are **incredibly made and maintained** using the food we eat and the oxygen we breathe. But just like the gingerbread man, get the **'ingredients'** or **'quantities'** wrong and our bodies can end up in a mess.

A good cook wouldn't make a mess of the gingerbread man because they would understand the characteristics of all the ingredients and the quantities required.

To maintain a **healthy body** and to protect it from harm requires **you** to be equally **knowledgeable** about the foods you eat and your general dietary requirements.

One of the reasons we eat, of course, is because our bodies need energy. Just like a motor car needs chemical energy in the form of petrol to make it move, so our bodies need chemical energy (from the food we eat) to enable us to move.

But energy is also used by the body to do other important things. It is used, for example, in the development and growth, maintenance and repair of all cells and body tissues including bone and muscle.

Now, energy is **measured in calories**, so knowing **how many calories** there are in a portion of food is very important.

Why?

Well, the problem with energy is if you supply the body with more energy than it needs (more calories), the body stores the excess energy as fat. But working out how much energy is in your food on a meal-by-meal basis is not always easy, so people tend not to bother. But that's when things can very quickly get out of hand.

So, what's the answer? Is there one?

Yes. Knowing **which kind of foods** contain lots of calories is the first lesson to learn. Having enough **discipline** to control how much you actually eat, meal by meal, is the next step. And finally, you need to **refrain from** eating high-calorie snacks between meals.

This all sounds like a lot of effort and not much fun!

Maybe, but it is very important if you want to keep a check on your weight and look after your health.

Getting to know your food

Just like the ingredients of a gingerbread man have their **purpose**, so do the different 'chemicals' in our **food**.

This, however, is **not something** that most people think about on a day-to-day basis. **Some people do**, of course: vegetarians and vegans, for example, make specific choices related to what they eat, and people with allergies and food intolerances have to be particularly careful with their diets. Some people (with eating disorders) struggle with eating at all.

As I'm sure you are aware, being overweight is a topic talked about a lot these days in the media and it is a very important topic. Being overweight as a teenager increases your risk of developing **diabetes** and other health conditions – and continued overweight in adulthood increases your chances of getting **heart disease**.

However, I'm not going to describe or discuss these health issues in detail here. If you are interested or have serious concerns related to any eating concerns or disorders, seek professional help by speaking to your doctor.

My aim is to help you to understand a bit more about the food you do eat.

Unless you are a **young carer**, chances are it's the **adults** in the family that do most of the food preparation. But that doesn't mean that you should just accept what you are given, without thinking about it.

So, **what do you know** about what you are eating?

What do you know about carbohydrates, proteins, minerals, vitamins and so on? All of which can end up on your plate in different forms, quantities and proportions.

Let's start with **carbohydrates**. What are they, why do we need them and what is their purpose? Well, let's investigate and see what we can discover, but we will do this on a 'need-to-know' basis, only (not too complicated).

What are carbohydrates? For our purposes, it is enough to know that carbohydrates are, in essence, **'sugars'**. Carbohydrates provide the body with **energy** and all of the cells in our body need energy.

Are they good for us?

Yes and no. There are 'good' carbs and there are 'not-so-good' carbs. But even the 'not-so-good' carbs are OK, if we don't overconsume them. Here are some examples of food products that **contain** carbohydrates: tomatoes, **dried fruit**, broccoli, **fruit juice**, asparagus, **some cereals**, brown rice, **sweets**, potatoes, **white bread**, oatmeal, **white rice**, bananas. You've probably guessed that the ones coloured **red** are the 'not-so-good' carbs.

OK, so some carbohydrates are good for us and some are not so good. Why is that?

To answer this question, you first need to be aware that there are **three types of carbohydrate.**

Now, whilst all carbohydrates are 'sugars', their chemical structures (which you do not need to understand) are **different** and it's this difference that **affects how our bodies are able to use them.**

Sugar, the type that is added to biscuits, chocolate, flavoured yoghurts, breakfast cereals, fizzy drinks and many other products, are called **free sugars.** This is one type of carbohydrate.

Starch is another carbohydrate. It is found in foods that come from plants. Starchy foods, such as bread, rice, potatoes and pasta, are examples.

Fibre is found in the **cell walls** of foods that come from plants. Good sources of fibre include fruit and vegetables, wholegrain bread, wholewheat pasta and pulses (beans and lentils).

OK – there are three different types of carbohydrate, they are found in different foods and their different 'structures' affect how our bodies are able to use them, yes?

Yes. Let me explain the last point. **Sugars,** such as fructose and glucose, because of their **very simple chemical structure, are easily and quickly used by the body to produce energy.** Rapidly rising blood sugar levels can be useful if you need a quick burst of energy, for example, but there can also be negative health effects if the body is exposed to too much sugar over long periods of time.

Starch, which has **a more complex chemical structure**, is 'broken down' to release energy **far more slowly by the body.** So, when you eat starchy foods, you can maintain your energy levels over a period of several hours.

And **fibre**, because of its **even more complex chemical structure, cannot be digested by the body at all.** However, as it passes through the body undigested, it helps regulate the body's **use of sugars**, helping to keep hunger and **blood sugar** in check.

So, how does this all link in with calories and being overweight?

Good question. You will remember that energy is measured in **calories** and, as we have just learnt, the body can 'release' energy from different carbohydrates at **different speeds.**

And as stated earlier, if you supply the body with more energy than it needs (or can use), **then the excess energy is stored in the body as fat.**

Unfortunately, the story doesn't end here. Carbohydrates are not the only 'enemy' when it comes to **calories.** Many foods that contain carbohydrates **also** contain **fat.**

It's clear that the story is now getting **rather complicated.** We need to simplify things if **you** are going to **look after your health** by **reducing your calorie intake** and thereby **prevent excessive weight gain.**

So, let's have a look at a **food label.**

Most food products (available in the shops today) carry a food label outlining what the product contains and in what proportions. So, reading the label is all you need to do to make sure you are in control of your food intake.

NUTRITION			GDA	
Typical values	per 100g	per pack	adult	per pack
Energy kJ	450	1345		
Energy kcal	105	315	2000	16%
Protein	7.5g	23.7g	45g	53%
Carbohydrate	8.8g	26.4g	230g	11%
Of which sugars	1.2g	3.6g	90g	4%
Fat	4.2g	12.6g	70g	18%
Of which saturates	2.7g	8.1g	20g	41%
Fibre	1.2g	3.6g	24g	15%
Sodium	0.24g	0.72g	2.4g	30%
Equivalent of salt	0.60g	1.80g	6.0g	30%
GDA = Guidance Daily Amount				

You must be joking?

Yes, I am joking. You only need to look at the example shown here to realise **how confusing food labels can be.**

Manufacturers are legally obliged to provide this information and using the 'traffic light' system – **red for high, green for low etc. – is helpful.**

The terms we have referred to so far (energy, sugar, starch, fibre etc.) do appear on food labels, but in a somewhat **confusing** manner in places.

Also provided on food labels is the **GDA** (Guidance Daily Amount). This refers to how much each ingredient contributes to the total amount that an **adult** should consume daily. Other labels use RI (Reference Intake), which has the same basic meaning. Look out for other 'wording' with similar meanings, too.

I am aware that some people will have a very good understanding of the information contained on food labels, but many may **not**. For the latter, I will attempt to create some clarity, but first I need to tell you about some of the other **important** 'substances' identified on food labels. These include **protein, minerals, vitamins** and **salt**.

Protein is an important component of every cell in the body. Hair and nails are mostly made of protein and our bodies use protein to **build and repair tissues** such as muscle.

Minerals are 'nutrients' used by the body to build bones and muscles as well as helping to regulate heartbeat, oxygenation of the body cells and blood clotting.

Vitamins are organic substances present in minute amounts in **natural foodstuffs**. They have numerous functions in the body including helping to fight off infection.

Sodium (salt) helps our body retain water and helps keep our blood pressure normal. It is important for the proper functioning of our muscles and so many other things.

You have probably realised by now, if you didn't know already, that what we all need to stay healthy is a **balanced diet**. A diet that contains everything the body needs and in the right proportions – just like the ingredients for a gingerbread man, or woman.

Ready meals (processed food)

Preparing your own food from scratch (using fresh produce) has got to be the best way to keep healthy in terms of 'knowing what you are eating'. But this can be time-consuming and more costly than buying ready meals.

Unfortunately, fifty per cent of the UK diet is now based on pre-prepared **processed foods** – the highest in Europe. These foods tend to contain less fibre and fewer vitamins than 'whole food' and often have a high salt, sugar and fat content.

So, what's the answer?

Good question. Put simply, what you need to do is:

1. Consume less processed food (if this is your habit).

2. Learn how to avoid the most 'damaging' processed foods.

Let's take a look at the food label below and see if we can clarify things.

We have learnt that carbohydrates are important for **energy** and that there are three types of carbohydrate: simple sugars, starch and fibre.

We also learnt that simple sugars are not so good for us. It's OK if we need a quick burst of energy (in exercise, for example), but if we consume too much during a 'sit-down' meal, the energy (the calories) just gets stored as fat.

Take a look at the right-hand column of this food label and notice that this particular product provides four per cent of our recommended daily amount (GDA) of simple sugar.

NUTRITION			GDA	
Typical values	per 100g	per pack	adult	per pack
Energy kJ	450	1345		
Energy kcal	105	315	2000	16%
Protein	7.5g	23.7g	45g	53%
Carbohydrate	8.8g	26.4g	230g	11%
Of which sugars	1.2g	3.6g	90g	4%
Fat	4.2g	12.6g	70g	18%
Of which saturates	2.7g	8.1g	20g	41%
Fibre	1.2g	3.6g	24g	15%
Sodium	0.24g	0.72g	2.4g	30%
Equivalent of salt	0.60g	1.80g	6.0g	30%
GDA = Guidance Daily Amount				

Not a lot, but this is just one part of a meal - puddings and drinks not included.

And then there is **fat**.
We haven't said very much about fat (in food products) so far, so let's take a quick look now. Many food items contain fat, but again there are different types: saturated, unsaturated and trans-fat.

Fat is essential for many bodily functions, as well as being a source of energy, but one type of fat, **saturated fat**, is not good for us **if we consume too much of it** – though it is essential in small amounts. While saturated fat is found naturally in many kinds of foods, it mainly comes from **animal sources** such as red meat, poultry and dairy products.

Look again at the right-hand column of the food label and you will see that this product contains forty-one per cent of the daily recommended amount of saturated fat. Once again, this is just one meal and it doesn't include a pudding.

Add to this milk on the breakfast cereals, lunchtime snacks, snack bars, drinks in the local café and this percentage can rise rapidly.

Now, let's give some thought to protein.

Put simply, protein is an important 'building block' of bone, muscle, cartilage, skin and blood – and foods that contain proteins also contain important vitamins. Protein, therefore, is extremely important for growth, development and immunity. Not getting enough protein in your diet, therefore, can lead to health issues, but so too can having **too much** protein (talk to your doctor on the **latter issue** for expert advice).

For our purpose here, getting the **right amount** of protein in your diet is what we need to be concerned with on a day-to-day basis.

Take a look at the food label again and notice that this product contains fifty-three per cent of the daily recommended amount of **protein (the GDA).**

Chicken and turkey breasts, eggs, cheese, tuna fish, cod, pulses, beans, lentils etc. are all good sources of protein.

NUTRITION			GDA	
Typical values	per 100g	per pack	adult	per pack
Energy kJ	450	1345		
Energy kcal	105	315	2000	16%
Protein	7.5g	23.7g	45g	53%
Carbohydrate	8.8g	26.4g	230g	11%
Of which sugars	1.2g	3.6g	90g	4%
Fat	4.2g	12.6g	70g	18%
Of which saturates	2.7g	8.1g	20g	41%
Fibre	1.2g	3.6g	24g	15%
Sodium	0.24g	0.72g	2.4g	30%
Equivalent of salt	0.60g	1.80g	6.0g	30%
GDA = Guidance Daily Amount				

And finally, **sodium.**

Sodium is another essential element that the body needs. The **problem with sodium is**: too much and this can lead to **hypertension** (high blood pressure), which is not good for the heart, and too little (very low levels) can also affect the heart. Sodium, therefore, is one of the most critical life-sustaining elements.

Most critical life-sustaining elements?

Yes, if you don't have enough sodium in your system, then you are at risk of becoming dehydrated (feeling very thirsty). Sodium is also important for the correct functioning of the digestive system and every cell in the body requires sodium in order to survive. It is also important for the proper functioning of your muscles, too – transmitting nerve impulses to trigger the muscles to contract and relax.

OK, sodium is important, but why is sodium 'linked to salt' on this food label?

Good question. **Sodium** occurs naturally in many food products in the form of sodium compounds or 'chemicals', but salt (sodium chloride) is also **added by producers** to act as a **preservative** in **processed foods**. Processed foods are those that have been 'treated' in various ways – they are not 'natural', as it were.

Salt is also **added** to processed foods **to make the ingredients taste better** (less bitter, for example).

So, let's be clear – **sodium**, which the body **does need** in **tiny amounts**, not only appears naturally in some food products, but is **also added by producers** to their products for the purposes explained above. Whatever you do, therefore, **don't add any more salt, from your saltshaker, to processed foods.**

Let's wrap this up!

Oh no, not another 'clever' title!

Sorry! Anyway, in the days when everybody prepared food 'from scratch' using natural fresh products, being concerned about 'creating a balanced diet' was less of an issue – it kind of happened naturally. Of course, many people today still do prepare meals from scratch, but not on a daily basis. Leading busy lives and the availability of pre-prepared meals and 'fast food' has had a big impact on what we eat.

If you **enjoy preparing and cooking food**, and have the **time** to do so and **sufficient income** to purchase the ingredients, then you are onto a winner in terms of your health. But let me make it clear, I do understand that many people struggle to find the money to buy healthy food items on a day-to-day basis. I am also aware that some people will have specific health conditions that can make weight control very difficult.

But for many others, 'convenience' is the cause. They have just fallen into the habit of buying and consuming **processed** or *'fast foods'* because it's quick and easy. However, the consumption of too much processed food is seriously damaging people's health.

Anyway, I hope the above information has been helpful, not only for you (**as a growing teenager**), but for the future (if you become a parent and have children of your own).

Let's talk exercise

Being naturally beautiful or handsome is something over which we have little control. Those characteristics might give you certain advantages in life, **but not necessarily**.

Being **healthy** in body and mind, however, is something over which most of us **do have some control** – and those characteristics, in the long-term, are more precious, more valuable and more beneficial than any outward features.

So why do people exercise?

Whilst some people **exercise** to **improve their body image** – slimmer waist, bigger muscles etc. – **exercise has many other benefits**. For example:

Some people exercise because they **really enjoy the feelings** it generates. It can lift their mood and create a sense of wellbeing.

Some people exercise to **relieve stress** – a chance to unwind after a busy day at school or work, for example.

Some people exercise because it's a **great way to socialise**. Running together, meeting friends at the gym, playing sport, or walking to and from school with friends are a few examples.

Some people exercise **to lose excess weight**.

Having spent some time getting to know your food and its benefits in the previous section, it's time (I think) to give some thought to the benefits of exercise.

OK!

If you're not a fan of exercise – you should read this!

To explain the full health benefits of exercise (if I could, which I can't) would require an entire book, but some of the basics are worth mentioning.

Exercise strengthens the lungs:

When you are **physically active**, your **lungs** need to **work harder** to supply the **additional oxygen** your muscles demand and exercise improves the lungs' ability to do this. Having healthy lungs means you can do more demanding physical activity without getting out of breath **quite as much**.

Exercise strengthens the heart muscles: Exercising **any** muscle increases its strength, and the heart **is a muscle**. You do know that the heart is a muscle?

Of course, we do – and it's not just a muscle, it's a pump.

I know, I'm only teasing – and you're right, it is a **pump**.

I forgot to say that.

Where was I? Oh yes, the heart, **which is a muscle**, has to work harder to supply the extra oxygen that your hard-working limbs demand when you are doing exercise. The **heart**, therefore, needs to **pump blood faster** and, in doing so, **the heart muscle itself** has to **work harder** and thereby **gets stronger**. Over time (and with increasing strength), the heart becomes more efficient and is able to **pump more blood with every beat**.

More blood with every beat!

As a result, the heart is better prepared to work hard when the body demands it. There is less stress on the heart and the surrounding blood vessels too, which reduces the risk of heart attack and other heart-related diseases.

Blood pressure

If you have ever pumped up a bicycle tyre with a hand pump, you will be aware of how hard it can be (with each stroke) to force air into the tyres. Imagine now **how much harder it would be** if that little rubber pipe (between the pump and the tyre) **deteriorated over time and got blocked with bits of old rubber.**

No problem; just throw it away and get a new one!

Unfortunately, when our blood vessels begin to get blocked as a result of the build-up of **plaque** (a fatty, waxy substance), not only is the supply of oxygenated blood to our heart and other tissues restricted, but our **blood pressure rises. Not such an easy problem to solve!**

High blood pressure can cause too many problems to list here. It's enough to say that the damage caused by high blood pressure can be **life-restricting and even life-threatening.**

So, like it or not – exercise is vital if you want to stay fit and healthy.

OK, let's hear it!

Walking fit

The **health of the nation** is a hugely complex picture and if you are interested in gaining an insight into life expectancy, 'everyday' health conditions, specific health conditions, regional variations, the effects of inequality on people's health and so much more, there are many internet sites providing a huge range of data (including .gov.uk sites).

Our knowledge surrounding healthcare issues and their consequences leaves no doubt that whilst the health of the population of the UK is generally good, **there are many concerns** that relate directly to our **lifestyles**.

Currently, in the UK, one in every seven people are gym members. Clearly, millions of people take their health and wellbeing seriously and there are countless outlets and internet sites selling everything from specialist sports clothing to home gym equipment – it's a multi-billion-pound industry.

But millions of people **don't want to go to a gym**, don't want to buy expensive exercise clothing or equipment, **but still need to look after their health**. So, what can they do? If nothing else, they can **walk** – it's a great all-round fitness activity. Walking is **free**; there are no gym fees or expensive clothing (except for a waterproof and some sturdy shoes).

But please remember, never walk alone at any time in a lonely location, even if the surroundings are familiar to you.

There's no getting away from it: Regular exercise is essential for your health and wellbeing.

Activities that are good for your health (physical and mental) include walking, cycling, running, swimming, playing football, gym activities, dancing and so on.

Activities that are **not so good for your health include** playing video games (for long periods), using an electric scooter, Internet surfing, TV watching (for long periods) and so on.

And before you say anything—

I wasn't going to!

OK. I know that I really didn't need to state the above because you knew it anyway. You did, didn't you? Well, most of you did, I'm sure!

Of course.

But maybe some of you, who do engage in the *least active* pastimes, do need to try to reduce your inactive periods and increase your physical activity.

But **it's your health, your choice.**

Now you are putting us under pressure.

Maybe, but only because I care – and so does the NHS.

Mental health

Mental health is a topic that receives a lot of attention in the media these days. Throughout history, of course, many people have suffered with mental health issues; but it wasn't something people (in general) talked about.

So, what is mental health?

Put simply, **mental health** is a **'state of mind'** determined by the processes taking place in the brain, which result in **thought**. What actually 'goes on in our heads' to produce thought, however, is hugely complex and doesn't need to concern us here other than to say – it's these 'goings-on' in our minds that are the essence of mental health.

'Goings-on' in our minds?

Absolutely. Most people would probably say that their **mental health was 'good'** if they felt a general **sense of wellbeing** – and, of course, having a general sense of wellbeing usually means that they are dealing quite well, in their minds, with life's challenges.

And let's not forget, our sense of wellbeing is reflected in our **relationships**, the things we **enjoy**, the things we **achieve**, the things that give us **comfort** and our **health**.

Now, since dealing with life's challenges requires **thought** (obviously), the process of **thinking** and the way we respond to those **thoughts** – either physically, emotionally or verbally – is so important.

Thoughts are fine and absolutely essential for life, but it's when these thoughts begin to disturb us that our mental health can begin to suffer.

It is clear, **but not necessarily easy to achieve,** that we are mentally healthier when we are 'in control' and can respond 'successfully' and 'appropriately' to life's difficult, challenging and ever-changing demands, but **we are all different** and don't always process our thoughts effectively.

Process our thoughts effectively? What do you mean?

I'll try to explain. Thoughts that enable us to function as human beings, both physically and mentally, that result in a **general feeling of wellbeing,** could be described as *'effective thoughts'.* They may be conscious thoughts (thoughts that we are aware of) or unconscious thoughts (thoughts that are hidden from our awareness).

Thoughts rarely exist in isolation. Indeed, a conscious thought (when we are alone) almost always demands a response; another thought and then another thought and then another. It's a bit like having a **conversation** or **discussion,** but we are having it with ourselves.

And it's this **conversation in the mind** – this interchange of thoughts – that we rely on to enable us to deal with those **everyday 'getting on with life' events** and those **not-so-pleasant, troubling events or situations,** which, if not resolved, are likely to impact negatively on our sense of wellbeing and, ultimately, our mental health.

Thoughts in action!

Some people in life appear to be so confident, easy-going, self-assured and able to cope with life's challenges with ease. Others (at times) struggle or fail to respond in a positive way to life's difficulties or unexpected distressing circumstances, and this can cause anxiety sometimes.

The above applies to people of all ages, of course, but it can be particularly challenging for a teenager.

After all, adolescence is a challenging time and a time of rapid change. You will experience changes in your body (the way your body looks and feels). You will experience changes in your relationships (your feelings related to social acceptance and independence) and you will experience changes related to your responsibilities (because you will be required to adapt to new demands and challenges). You will also likely experience changes in the way you think and how this affects your beliefs and opinions.

The thing about change is that it can take a bit of getting used to.

Through lack of experience, you will (understandably) sometimes say the wrong thing or get things wrong. And to make matters worse, with your newfound 'confidence', you may sometimes come over as selfish or disrespectful.

Have you finished?

Nearly, but I'm not trying to upset you. I do understand.

As I have said before, navigating the teenage years is a bit like baking a cake without a recipe.

Anxiety, in the teenage years, is to be expected. The problem with anxiety is that as well as being **horrible to experience** at the time, if it's not addressed it can **lead to depression,** with all the consequences this can have for your mental health. **Anxiety** can result from **numerous different causes,** including uncertainty, despair, embarrassment, disappointment, shame, humiliation, relationship break-ups, loneliness, bullying, sexual abuse, physical pain and so on.

Life, for most people is a roller coaster of ups and downs, pleasure and disappointment, good luck and misfortune, and we accept this as 'just life'. But some of the 'downs', if not addressed successfully, can be the beginning of an avalanche of distressing and confusing thoughts that can make the original issue, or concern, more difficult to resolve. So, how can you begin to help yourself, how could you proceed?

For some people, a visit to the **doctor** may be necessary and medication, therapy or counselling may be prescribed – of course, **some** mental health conditions **can only be addressed using these methods**. But with thought, effort and determination, many young people will be able to help themselves. As suggested above, our 'sense of wellbeing' is reflected in our **Relationships,** the things we **Enjoy,** the things we **Achieve,** the things that give us **Comfort** and our **Health.**

Knowing what is troubling you will be very personal to yourself and will likely impact on a number of R, E, A, C and H situations.

So often, the best thing to do (if you can) is to address and sort out **one issue at a time** – starting with the least demanding, least stressful issue. Then, move on to the next least demanding, least stressful issue and so on. With this approach, you should be able to declutter your mind, which should make sorting out the bigger issues that bit easier. So, with the above in mind, give some thought to the following.

Motives and motivations

Mental health is clearly a complex, multi-faceted 'condition' and this is not surprising since life itself is, well, complex (to say the least) – and whilst **thoughts determine our emotions and behaviours, life's events, of course, influence both**.

At a very simplistic level, human activity can be placed into three categories:

1. The things we enjoy doing or want to do.

2. The things we don't particularly want to do but are the necessities of life.

3. The things we have to deal with in life, caused by unexpected events, or difficult and challenging circumstances.

OK, I get the picture, but so what?

Well, with regards to the first and second points, we almost always **plan** for these events.

In the case of the first point:

We might **plan** an evening out with friends, a visit to the cinema, a date with a girlfriend or boyfriend, a trip or holiday and so on. **It's the natural thing to do.** Planning helps us to 'get things right' to enable us to make the most of our lives.

In the case of the second point: Planning ensures that we **have what we need in place,** either in the short term or long term, to make **what we want to do (or have to do) doable.**

But what about the third point? It's very difficult to plan for events or circumstances in the future **that we cannot possibly predict in advance,** and that **might or might not happen anyway.** And yet, these are some of the very events or circumstances that are likely to cause anxiety when they occur and can be the 'instigators' of mental ill-health.

So, is there anything **you should be aware of,** or **anything you could do,** to **help you to be more prepared** for such eventualities and possibly help to minimise the potential onset of mental ill-health when faced with anxiety-provoking situations? **Let's find out.**

Many influences combine to make us who we are. Furthermore, mental health is not 'consistent'. Different circumstances create different challenges and emotions that can require different responses. In this context, the concepts of 'personality' and 'intelligence' **may** have a part to play. After all, as we mentioned earlier:

Some people in life appear to be **so confident, easy-going, self-assured** and able to cope with life's challenges with ease. Others (at times) struggle or fail to respond in a positive way.

But just to complicate things even more, it has to be acknowledged that there are many factors that can impact on our mental health **over which we have little or no control** including genetics (inherited characteristics), personal circumstances (e.g., the home environment), life experiences (e.g., trauma or abuse) and family history (e.g., mental health problems). For the moment, let's give some thought to personality and intelligence.

Personality

I like to think of personality as the combination of characteristics, qualities, patterns of thinking, feelings and behaviours that makes a person unique.

I'll go with that!

Previously, we took a brief look at some identifiable positive and negative characteristics and considered how they might affect the way one individual **might** relate to another.

Whilst relating well to our fellow human beings has got to be beneficial in terms of our mental health, relating to (or reacting to) challenging or distressing situations in a positive way should also be beneficial.

Clearly, some individuals are 'better than others' in dealing with either of the above situations. You might say that it's down to their personality, but personality is a complex subject.

Even so, some individuals do appear to have personality characteristics that appear to benefit them in different situations whilst others have characteristics that appear to disadvantage them.

Having a stable personality – not being prone to extremes of thought or behaviour – is usually considered an advantage in terms of mental health.

Which of the characteristics listed below do you think are likely to be displayed by an individual with a stable personality?

Loving, argumentative, generous, reliable, humble, confident, impatient, considerate, lazy, optimistic.

You don't want me to list them, do you? It's obvious.

OK, but what about yourself. Would you say that you had a stable personality? If so, great, but if not, is this something you need to think about?

This is getting rather personal! True, but being aware of your own strengths and weaknesses should help you to navigate your own R, E, A, C and H challenges more successfully.

___

And what about intelligence? Do you fancy giving a bit of thought to this subject?

As long as you don't get too personal!

OK. It may be stating the obvious, but:

If we are **unable** to respond to and sort out upsetting circumstances in life, then we are **likely** to remain upset. But if we are **able** to respond to and sort out upsetting circumstances in life, then we are **less likely** to be upset.

OK, so are you suggesting that my intelligence might be an issue here?

Not necessarily the kind of intelligence you might be thinking about – just bear with me.

If you look up the meaning of intelligence, you will find a variety of **definitions**. A simple one states that 'intelligence is **the ability to understand, learn and work things out effectively**'. But the ability to understand, learn and work things out effectively can relate to **so many different circumstances**. People can be 'intellectually' really good at doing all sorts of different things in their academic life, social life, work life, family life and so on.

But there is one 'intellectual ability' that is potentially very beneficial in helping to manage our mental health – and that is **'emotional intelligence'. Emotional intelligence** can be described as 'the ability to **understand** our own emotions and the emotions of others, and the **ability to** regulate and manage those emotions'. Well, that all sounds **fairly straightforward**.

Straightforward? You're joking!

Yes, I am. To understand **our own emotions**, and regulate and manage those emotions, we need an effective **self-awareness** (an **understanding we have** – or think we have – about ourselves, our limitations and capabilities, our likes and dislikes). Whilst **self-awareness** can be a very valuable asset, **it isn't always effective** because it doesn't always enable us to **see the truth** about ourselves.

For example: If (because of your self-awareness) you have 'come to the belief' **that you are a failure**, you need to challenge that assumption, because it's almost certainly not true and based on unrealistic self-criticism.

Emotional intelligence? Self-awareness? This is all getting rather complicated!

It is a little, but all you need to remember about self-awareness is this: **irrational self-awareness** (self-awareness that is **not logical** and therefore not based on sound reasoning) can be very destructive and make one's ability to deal with life's demands less likely to be successful.

And with regard to **emotional intelligence**, just remember that every human being is unique (even identical twins). We think differently; we behave differently; we see life differently.

That's true!

_____

And this is when **emotional intelligence** – the ability to *'understand'* how our own thinking and emotions **can affect others** (as well as ourselves) – can impact on our mental health – if we 'mess thing up'.

So, just consider this:

1. Other people are likely to have different views and/or beliefs to yourself.

2. Other people will have different likes and dislikes to yourself.

3. Different personalities can impact on an individual's thoughts and behaviour.

We are all (like it or not) **emotional beings**, but – as we have just alluded to – we are not all the same. We may, for example, recognise feelings of happiness, sadness, joy, anger, shame, embarrassment, excitement and so on, but the way we experience all, or any of these, will likely be different.

Now, whilst respecting **our own values, beliefs, needs and desires** in life is important, it is when these **conflict with** the values, beliefs, needs and desires **of others** that problems can arise. If we can accept, understand and respect this, and adapt our behaviour accordingly, then life has the potential to be so much better for all of us – and this can only be good for our own and other people's mental health.

So where do we go from here?

Well, I suggest we have a look at the 'Why, What, When strategy'.

The – what? – strategy?

No, the 'Why, W…' – oh! You were joking.

The Why, What, When strategy

As suggested above, **distress** has a tendency to **cloud our thinking** and we are often not in the best 'frame of mind' to deal with difficult situations as they arise. In fact, **lack of forethought** can sometimes make the problem worse – if you overreact or, at the other extreme, do nothing.

I know that sometimes you can be so overwhelmed with an issue or issues that are troubling you that you feel incapable of helping yourself at all. I know! But ideally you should (if you can) **try** to calm down and when you feel able, ask the question 'Why?'. **Why** has this thing happened, or **why** do I feel this way? Knowing **why** something has happened is usually (but not always) fairly obvious, but **understanding why** something has happened is often much more difficult to determine or accept.

If you are going to resolve an issue, or issues that are disturbing you, and avoid the long-term potential 'damage' to your mental health, something (usually) has to change. But things can only begin to change if you are very clear in your mind what needs to change. **Understanding why** something has occurred requires you **to be very honest with yourself** and this is where emotional intelligence, the ability to 'understand' how our own thinking and emotions **can affect others** (as well as ourselves), is so valuable.

No, the 'Why, W...' – oh! You were joking.

The truth may have been the result of a mistake, misjudgement, selfishness – any number of causes – but if it was your fault, you must be prepared to accept it and decide how to proceed.

The 'what' question

Knowing why the issue, the problem, the event, the situation (or whatever) happened and **understanding why** it happened should ideally lead you to ask yourself the 'what' question – '**What** to do next?' Because unresolved issues can fester in the mind and these can sometimes have long-term damaging consequences.

'What to do next?', of course, will be dependent on whether the fault was yours or someone else's. Often you will be able to work out 'what to do next' **yourself** and this can be very beneficial sometimes.

Indeed, the greater **your understanding** of the issue and the greater **your determination** to satisfactorily resolve the issue, then the greater the chance of long-term benefits. Not only will you have gained **valuable experience**, but you will also have increased your **self-confidence**, too.

But if you genuinely just don't know why you feel so low, or how to proceed, or if you feel so dispirited (for whatever reasons) and you fear that you are at risk (in any way), then getting help straightaway is so important. This could be help from a teacher or your school counselling service or calling a **helpline**.

Remember, ChildLine – telephone number: 0800 1111 – will get you through to a counsellor, who will listen and support you with anything you'd like to talk about.

Finally, the **'when'** bit happens when you feel confident that are ready to act.

The sooner, the better is probably the best option, but that's not always possible or appropriate. The old saying 'Never put off till tomorrow what you can do today' is (I think) very appropriate when it comes to issues that trouble the mind.

So just remember, mental health problems can arise very quickly, but overcoming them can take much longer and dwelling on issues (going **over and over** upsetting circumstances) can very easily drag you down into a state of unmanageable depression.

If it's helpful, therefore, use the 'Why, What, When strategy' and I'm sure that you will be surprised at just how empowering it can be to know that:

You can confidently **look after yourself.**

You can **resolve issues yourself.**

You can **reduce the negative effects** of life's inevitable difficult experiences.

Well, that's it. I hope you have enjoyed our conversations and that the topics covered have been useful.

Goodbye then and good luck in your future lives.

James Garratt

Index

Index

Index

REACH when all is said and done

The teenage years are such a special time, when **relationships** of yours and mine, reflect the qualities (or not) which can dictate our future lives or lot.
A time to grow, a time to change, a time to experience decisions made.
But get it right and hope will be, a brighter future for you and me.

Enjoyment is ours to share; as long as we respect and care.
Anxiety, fear, rejection, depression - what place have these if we have compassion?
To bully, to threaten, to racially or sexually abuse, surely these are not behaviours one would willingly choose?
Be pleasant, be kind, give all due respect or you'll find that your conscience will demand you reflect.
With friends who support you, the responsible kind, there'll be fun there'll be laughter and joy to be found.
Cherish those friendships and with compromise, you'll ensure that enjoyment for all will abound.

A time to do your very best - so let **achievement** be the test. From listening, thinking and understanding you'll soon progress to problem solving.
And then despite the odds, with dedication and efforts made, you can show what you have gained.
But the path ahead is yours to choose - get it wrong and you will lose.
Time is no more - once time is lost - and to catch up later comes at such a cost.
Choose wisely then, your future beckons, don't let regrets your prospects threaten.

We all need time to relax and to feel **comfort** in our lives and tasks, to satisfy our needs and wants - but never to be dispensed - at someone else's, or our own, expense.

Find time to give, find time to share, find time to love support and care.

In times of need, when friends are low that's when your comfort needs to show.

Words of support with empathy reflected, should help their emotions to be detected.

Be kind, be gracious, be none-judgemental, the comfort journey must be gentle.

Good **health** can be a lottery - a random chance, not clear to see, but when you have the chance to choose, take great care that you do not abuse.

Your health (of course) your choice (respected) but get it wrong will you accept it?

You need to know the risks you're taking; but you do of course, there's no mistaking.

Not least of course are affairs of the heart. Don't be rushed or persuaded, don't be forced to take part.

Enjoy, be happy, be cautious be wise, savour the years and learn from the start, that decisions made and actions taken, if made in haste can leave lives broken.

Matador